Dedication:

This book is dedicated to all those who strive for financial empowerment, and to those who believe that with the right knowledge and mindset, anyone can achieve lasting financial success. May this book serve as a catalyst for your financial transformation and bring you the confidence you seek.

Copyright Statement:

Contents

Preface

 This book is the culmination of decades of learning, carefully organized to create a seamless and engaging experience. Will you join me on this transformative journey, starting from the beginning and progressing toward a brighter future?

From an early age, I've been captivated by the stark disparities between the wealthy and the typical working class. Witnessing the tireless efforts of individuals who, despite their determination, only achieved modest results, left me disheartened by the injustices of such a system. It ignited an insatiable curiosity within me to uncover the underlying reasons behind this divide. While ordinary people possess the potential to create lasting wealth, they often lack the necessary knowledge and planning, leading to unpredictable outcomes.

While this book doesn't provide personalized financial advice, its purpose is to expand your awareness of the limitless possibilities to create wealth for you and future generations; point you in the right directions.

Going beyond conventional wealth planning, this book delves into the crucial element of human factors. By choosing to engage with these pages, you have already demonstrated the essential ingredient for improving your circumstances: the courage to take action. Wealth, though rooted in the heart and mind, requires tangible manifestation through decisive steps; action.

Even if you currently have limited resources, you have the potential to amass a fortune during your lifetime. According to an HSBC advertisement, 67% of billionaires created their own success from humble beginnings.

Without a well-defined plan and unwavering motivation, the pursuit of wealth remains elusive and even if achieved, its preservation becomes uncertain. Fortunately, the information presented in this book is carefully crafted to guide you toward the path of millionaire status and continued growth.

Personally, I come from a wealthy family, yet my father's support was limited during various stages of my life. He wanted me to stand on my own two feet, which provided a comfortable lifestyle at home but lacked crucial financial guidance. I encountered challenges along the way and learned from them. While my initial attempts at success faced setbacks due to my insistence on independence, I discovered that there are faster paths to wealth once we overcome negative psychological patterns. Thankfully, numerous resources exist to help us break free from the limitations ingrained in our minds. In the course of my journey, friends have witnessed positive changes in my attitude, all thanks to the teachers I've encountered.

Together, let us embark on this transformative journey, as I share the knowledge and insights gained over the years.

Forward

by Susan Pratt

I've known Allen for many years. He asked me to write this introduction because I was a professor for many years and can relate to young adults. Allen has teenage and young adult children but also wanted to pass along his knowledge to a broader audience. So I offered to help edit this book and give feedback. I can also relate to the information here and how it could have been influential to me when I was younger.

When I was a young girl I had chores to do and earned an allowance. My parents would buy me clothes, but if I wanted a pair of Levi's Jeans I had to save my money and purchase them myself. Once I turned 12 I started my first official job babysitting. My parents steered me to open a bank account to start saving money. They also instilled the importance of getting an education. They were amazing and I am truly grateful for them and the knowledge they gave me was limited to what they learned.

If I was a parent I would be asking my teenage children what desires, goals, or dreams they had. Moreover, I would be teaching them about entrepreneurship and working for themselves instead of "climbing the corporate ladder." Why be "bossed" around by someone else when you can be your own boss? Additionally, I would emphasize always asking for help/information/guidance when needed. The answer is ALWAYS no if you don't ask. A simple request could open up doors beyond your wildest dreams.

Learn to manifest and envision the life you want to create. Money is a tool, use it with positive energy and always continue to learn and grow. Use the information in this book to guide you in your financial abundance. Remember…every master was once a disaster. Now go create a masterpiece called your life!

1
The Way Forward

Self-Serve Universe

We may not like it or we may love that it is a self-serve universe. What is a self-serve universe you ask? That means it's up to us how most of our life turns out. As individuals, we get to choose or create our reality or our destiny in life. Yes, we were raised by people when we were babies into adulthood and then we became more free to make our own decisions. The adults that raised us fade into the background and get on with their own lives mostly. We're out of the house finally and free! But oops, we have to earn money.

Once we become an adult then most of what we do is up to us as a choice. Most of our needs are looked after by ourselves. There are of course people that have trust funds or wealthy parents and unfortunately, they may not realize that it's still up to them to look after their finances. Money is a tool. The key or goal is to use that money "tool" wisely to create more freedom. More money does not always mean more freedom. As we'll find out later you could have a lot of money to start out with and as some celebrities have demonstrated they can become bankrupt and homeless.

Some religions speak about how God looks after the birds. I've noticed that the birds gather their own food and build their nests. I'm just saying that even when some people say the birds don't need to "toil", that's not what I've seen, and the same for people that are wealthy or homeless and everything in between. Somebody had to do something to have that amount of money and status.

Money does establish boundaries for our choices in life. We might not afford a ride on a spaceship or submarine, but it's just glamor usually. The essential things are feeling good and having plenty of choice in where we live and what we do. Essentially, money must not be the "pursuit of happiness!" Happiness is a choice and money is a tool to create your freedom of things that are important to you!

Retirement Happens

As a teenager I didn't care about retirement or most of the things that adults did. I thought it was irrelevant to my life. I was like most teenagers believing that I was smarter than all those adults, and of course, retirement just seems too far away. Why would I worry about that?

As I got older and started working, I realized that there was going to be a time when I would retire. I probably would reach the age of 65, and at that point, I would need to not have a job and hopefully enjoy retirement. We've all seen elderly people working at Walmart. They didn't want to do that job. They did it out of necessity. It's because they didn't have someone guiding them in financial planning. That's an important distinction and that's why I'm hoping you will read to the end of this book.

Retirement living standards are just our choices being expressed over time. If we make better choices our freedoms in retirement are greater. Retiring early, with enough money, happens for many people that make better choices.

Savings, Really?

Savings is the power that builds early retirements. Retirement means doing **what** you want, **when** you want **without** anyone stopping you. True freedom because you have time and money to live life on your terms.

The term "living paycheck to paycheck" typically refers to individuals or households who rely on each paycheck to cover their normal expenses like rent or food, and have very little or no savings. And if nothing else changes in their plans, they could end up being a Walmart greeter: "Hey, did you know I made $100,000 per year and spent it all?" Of course, that's not what the greeters are told to say.

Most teenagers don't like numbers. And our education system fails to educate them about financial growth and investments. Whether you like them or not, numbers create bank accounts, loans, and interest and have either a positive or negative effect on the outcome of your life in this high-speed economic world. Hundreds of years ago with the barter system, when we traded goats and eggs, numbers didn't matter so much. We're not going back there, and would you really want to? No. So here we are in a digital world and your personal numbers won't act like great friends…numbers don't forgive and forget as good friends do.

The Savings Equation: Income - Bills - Vanity = Savings.

Income is money that comes to you from a job, a business, or residual income.
Bills are ALL the payments that create your existence and the essentials you must have to stay alive.
Vanity is things that you want to have that are not necessary but are purchased for temporary pleasure. Older people may use words like vanity or ego-driven. Many teenagers use the term "flex" to refer to showing off possessions, achievements, or lifestyle. It's always related to material possessions, physical appearance, or social status.

Vanity items seem necessary, and "why not?" They are the pretty things that make us feel better. We want them all. The latest new phone for example.

The strange "selfish power" of vanity is it runs the personal economy for billions of people. I've seen about 40% of people making $100,000 per year living paycheck to paycheck. They're basically broke in a month unless they keep working. They should have some money in the bank but don't. Why not?

Vanity is always the robber in plain sight that they don't see, and you can't tell them. They can't hear you even if you say something. This is like watching a horror movie.

Enough *isn't* Enough, until it is Enough

When vanity drives us there is no stopping in spending. The Hollywood celebrities that made millions and then became bankrupt and homeless are real people. They had it all and probably won't be recovering from the despair of losing it all and being permanently poor.

In a self-serve universe, nobody is required to save them. They did it to themselves. Vanity was in control, and they are stuck in a mid-life pit of hell. They didn't think they'd end up like some horror movie character: poor and suffering. The monster they didn't see was their spending habits and lack of building sustainable wealth for their retirement freedom.

Some people will always have more money than you have. But they might not be happier if they are actively pursuing more and more. The attainment of happiness is a personal choice. "I have enough." As mentioned earlier, the "pursuit of happiness" is a misguided meme. Being happy while pursuing a goal is constant fulfillment. "I'm not there yet but I'm on the path."

Some of the grumpiest people I know are wealthy. They **never** have enough and they are never happy with what they have. No thanks! In some religious traditions, they know that one path to happiness is gratitude. Grateful for having breath and choice and appreciation for what they have. By that definition, the never-enough crowd can't actually be happy. I've had them tell me "I'm happy," but still listen to them criticize and complain about things. Complaining doesn't convince me they're truly happy or grateful.

Compound Numbers don't lie

Numbers don't lie unless they are presented falsely. If numbers don't lie, then we can give them our attention. For example, the money in a wallet comes and goes. You probably know roughly how much is in there. Money in the bank or digital wallet (like cryptocurrency) is easy to look up. If you have credit cards or other pay-later agreements, those are reviewable too. But there is another subtle number that sneaks up on most people: compounding.

Here's how compounding works. If you borrow money, you pay back the money and interest on that loan. The company that loaned you that money loves the interest payment. Institutions like banks don't spend that interest payment. It's like dessert for them. Banks are smart about money. They will take the interest and lend that out too. Then they get interest on the interest. It's nothing much in the beginning but over many years, it becomes serious money.

Here's a table showing the principal and interest for a $1,000 investment with a 10% interest rate over different time periods: (see appendix for detailed calculations)

Year	Principal	Compound Interest
1	$1,000	$100
2	$1,000	$610
10	$1,000	$1,593
15	$1,000	$4,177
20	$1,000	$6,727

In the first year, the interest earned is $100, which is calculated by multiplying the principal ($1,000) by the interest rate (10%).

After 5 years, the interest is $610, which includes both the initial interest earned and the compounded interest over the years. The compounded interest is calculated based on the principal and the accumulated interest from previous years.

Similarly, the interest for 10 years, 15 years, and 20 years takes into account the compounding effect, resulting in higher interest amounts over time. The key aspect of compounding is now you are making money on interest. How great is that?

Strange things happen if you increase the interest rate by 5% more.

Here are the two rates side by side.

Year	Principal	Interest at 10%	Interest 15%
1	$1,000	$100	$150
5	$1,000	$610	$1,070
10	$1,000	$1,593	$4,046
15	$1,000	$4,177	$9,962
20	$1,000	$6,727	$19,498

15% interest is not twice 10%. It's another half (50% more than 10%). But the compounded numbers start running away and become triple the outcome. Numbers don't lie. They are either working for you or against you.

iPhone or Apple

This is where we see how compounding can work for us and vanity works against other people.

I started this "Money School" for my teenagers and I asked them if they knew someone that had more than one iPhone. Of course, they knew a parent that had many iPhones. We looked at that choice in detail to become wiser than that parent.

We are assuming the price of the iPhone without a contract. The contract means they are paying for the phone in installments. We looked up the prices for the iPhone on the internet.

Question	Answer
When did they buy the first one?	2011
How much did they spend on their first iPhones?	The first one was $800
When did they buy the next one?	2013
How much did they spend on their next iPhone?	Over $800.
How many iPhones do they have?	5
Do their old phones work?	Yes. He just likes having the latest one.

If we got a new phone every 4 or 5 years instead of more often, here's the difference: 2 x $800 = $1,600. Versus 5 x $800 = $4,000. So what? Let's presume that we used the money to buy shares in the company *Apple* instead of another phone. We have saved $2,400.

The price of *Apple* shares changes over time. The value of the company *Apple* is increasing, meanwhile the old phones sit in a drawer and lose value over time.

Here we didn't spend more money. We just did *different* things with our money:

Buying Shares in Apple Co.	Shares Bought with $	Total Shares Owned
2012: $20/share	$800 / 20 = 40 shares	40
2015: $30/share	$800 / 30 = 26.6 shares	66.6
2018 $45/share	$800 / 45 = 17.7 shares	84.3

We used $2,400 to buy shares of the company instead of buying their products. In May 2023, the value of *Apple* shares was $165 per share. Our shares are worth $41,134. You can guess what the iPhones in the drawer are worth; much less than $2,400. We still spent the same $4,000 in those 10 years but with very different results by choosing more lucrative choices. Knowledge and choices can make a massive difference in our retirement savings. Instead of the fleeting vanity from the latest phone and a drawer full of useless gadgets, we have serious long-term money in the bank.

Corporate owner, shareholder, worker

In your self-serve universe, you need to pay your bills. There's no shame in having a job. Paying your way is something to be proud of. But not too proud either since it's just a normal requirement of life.

Homeless people often have unresolved psychological issues and typically can't change their futures. The rest of us can make choices and work on our futures. Changing jobs, or starting a small business are within our reach. Learning better ways to invest our time and money is within our reach too.

Investing or Trading

Many people think about investing in their careers or shares of a company or relationships. I'm suggesting that everything is a trade. We only should hang onto some things for a while, and not permanently. This is an advanced topic so I'll only cover the introduction to it here.

If something is good for us, then we should hang on to it. But not hang onto things that are turning bad for us. We often hang on to something as a habit. For example, what if the old cellphone is sold and shares in Apple were bought? That's financially better.

I review everything that I'm holding periodically. Of course, some things might be a year before I question myself if it's still good for me.

Other things might be every month or when an event happens. That's all.

Trading stock shares means I would hold something for a while expecting its value to increase for basic reasons. If it's not working out, I'll sell those shares and buy something else.

Salespeople will tell you to "invest" in something but they really want you to buy something. This is slippery sales talk. In my response, I'd ask them "What will it be worth in 5 years? (as an investment)." That's where the truth comes out about it being an investment or not.

Investing in a career with education is usually a good idea. The value of that investment is probably going to help with the money you earn. The cost of the investment is easy. But see If you can figure out the value of the investment over time. How much more money will I make? If they're selling education, how do you know those long-term results are right? Numbers don't lie.

Motivation

If you lack motivation, remember that poverty sucks. The choices poor people have makes some of them slip into crime. In contrast, if you have money, you can be a positive influence. Money gives you more choices, not more happiness. The ideal level is the freedom that you can create.

Chapter Summary

Our choices and actions largely determine our lives. As we transition into adulthood, the responsibility for our needs and finances falls on us, regardless of any potential advantages like trust funds or wealthy parents. Money is a tool that, when used wisely, can provide freedom and choices. Retirement planning and making good financial decisions ensure a comfortable future.

The role of gratitude is finding contentment and fulfillment. But pursuing more and more wealth doesn't deliver happiness. Excessive spending is a trap too. In the next chapters, we see the sources of happiness versus pleasure. We can look at careers and their impact on happiness and income.

Chapter Appendix - Detailed Calculations

Here are the detailed calculations for the first 10 years, assuming a principle of $1,000 and an annual interest rate of 10% compounded annually:

Year	Beginning Balance	Interest Earned	Ending Balance
1	$1,000.00	$100.00	$1,100.00
2	$1,100.00	$110.00	$1,210.00
3	$1,210.00	$121.00	$1,331.00
4	$1,331.00	$133.10	$1,464.10
5	$1,464.10	$146.41	$1,610.51
6	$1,610.51	$161.05	$1,771.56
7	$1,771.56	$177.16	$1,948.72
8	$1,948.72	$194.87	$2,143.59
9	$2,143.59	$214.36	$2,357.95
10	$2,357.95	$235.80	$2,593.75

The total is $2,593: the original $1,000 plus the $1,593 of interest becomes $2,593. This matches the numbers earlier. It only goes to the 10-year mark but you get the idea now.

In each year, the interest earned is calculated by multiplying the beginning balance by the interest rate. The other tables highlight the total interest earned to demonstrate the power of compounding interest. We really did start with only $1,000 and how that grew with time on its side.

The interest earned starts to get dramatic at 30 and 40 years. Getting past the first 5 years is the biggest hurdle for most beginners. You saw what $2,400 investing in Apple did. That was in only 11 years.

Seriously! Some people have become millionaires through a simple investing plan that they stuck with.

I've watched a lot of fakers say they made a fortune, but haven't seen the numbers to back up their claims. Here you have the numbers that any calculator can verify for you.

2
Three Assets You Already Have Forever

We all start out with three assets in life: time, relationships, and health. You already use these three assets and they're always yours. Sometimes, you can trade those assets for things like money. Sometimes we trade one asset for a different asset. For example, we use some time to improve our relationships. I call them assets because they're yours to use and control.

The most common way adults trade their time is for money at a job. It's called work generally because most people are dissatisfied with the work that they do. Many adults didn't spend enough time figuring out what would be a good job or career for themselves. I know a man that started part-time as a teenager at a fast-food place and then eventually became a manager. When asked why he was the manager, he says that's where I started.

Many other people didn't have the opportunity of more choices that can come from having higher skills. Perhaps their parents were poor and they couldn't afford a better education for their children. Unfortunately, some children also did not have emotional guidance or support about future success tips related to education or finances.

There are millions of people that have the similar three assets that you have today. As you know, it's also a very connected world. I have great respect for people that invent things, writers, and many service providers. They are a positive influence and they live their autonomous lives. They help me indirectly and I'm grateful for those anonymous, autonomous people. I could never thank them all individually. That's both sides of being in a highly connected, but also separated economy.

Time is Money If You Say So

It's your life. You can use your time to earn money. You also have the choice to spend time being a family member and looking after and raising children, or supporting an elderly person. Your life and how you live it is yours to choose.

If someone tells you "Time is money" they've told you a lot about their personal values and objectives. I listen to what they say and try to determine what they meant. When I was younger, I would react to what they said, as if it was a command or something. As if I was being disrespectful of their time or money. Now I just listen objectively and step out of their way. Each person has the right to express their views and values.

Everything is a Trade

In Chapter 1, I said that I review things periodically to see what I'm holding to determine whether or not I need to change anything. This is event-based or condition-based. I have no idea what the future holds, nor can I predict anything.

I will change what I'm doing and who I meet based on events or conditions. But I always remember and prioritize that it's my choice and results by taking action or not taking action when things change.

Management by Walking Around

Based on a true story from the Switzerland farming community of many years ago. The farmer died and the farmer's wife didn't know what to do. The farmer's sudden passing left his wife uncertain and overwhelmed. Seeking guidance, she turned to the wise local priest, who revealed a plan left by her husband for such a tragic occasion. His instructions were simple but a little mysterious too.

"Take this small box," the priest said, placing it gently in her hands. "Wear it around your neck and walk the perimeter of your vast farm every day for a year."

Intrigued by the enigmatic advice, the farmer's wife agreed to embark on this unusual journey. With the box hanging around her neck, she began her daily walks, observing everything around her with newfound curiosity, not fear.

As the days turned into weeks, she started noticing things she had never paid attention to before. She engaged in conversations with the farmhands, asking questions and learning from their experiences. Slowly but surely, she started unraveling the various operations of the farm.

Within a year's time, she had become an expert in running the farm. She knew the best time to plant and harvest, how to care for the livestock, and how to maintain the delicate balance of nature within their large farmland. The once-uncertain farmer's wife had transformed into a capable and knowledgeable steward of the farm.

When the year finally came to an end, she felt a mix of excitement and apprehension. It was time to unlock the mystery inside the box. With trembling hands, she opened it, expecting a profound revelation.

To her surprise, nestled within the box was a beautifully crafted key made of solid gold. Its intricate engravings seemed to hold a secret of their own. Alongside the key was a note, written by her late husband, explaining its significance.

"My love," the note read, "this key represents the wisdom and strength you have gained through your dedicated efforts. It is the key to unlocking the prosperity hidden within our farm, and the key to unlocking your own potential. Embrace it, cherish it, and may it guide you on your journey to a bright future."

Gazing at the key, she felt a surge of determination and self-belief. It symbolized the trust her husband had in her abilities, and she was determined to prove him right. Armed with the newfound knowledge and the golden key, she set out to implement innovative techniques and transformative ideas on the farm.

Word of her success spread far and wide, attracting attention from young farmers and aspiring entrepreneurs alike. She became a beacon of inspiration, sharing her wisdom and mentoring others to unlock their own hidden potential.

Years later, as she passed the farm's reins to the next generation, the farmer's wife held onto the box and its golden key as a reminder of the transformative journey she had undertaken. It served as a testament to the power of perseverance, curiosity, and the incredible strength that resides within each of us, waiting to be discovered.

Your life is a collection of choices that produce results. You can change your choices and eventually get different results and sometimes making a change is not easy. Most people don't walk around their 'farm' to see what should be done. It is all about awareness. Awareness is the key, which may turn into habits that serve us. Do you look before you cross the street? Of course, you do.

When I'm asked by youngsters, "Why should I brush my teeth?" It's a logical question. I reply "Just brush the ones you want to keep." Then they can decide what to do, instead of being forced; without any reasoning. It makes them smarter, not slaves. They choose the habit based on information. In the same way, we all have habits that serve us and we can observe their overall impact on our lives.

It Doesn't Exist Outside of Time

In life if something isn't part of our schedule, it's unlikely to become a reality. It's similar to the habit of brushing our teeth – we do it consistently because it's ingrained in our routine. I had an acquaintance who would often say, "I'm going to win the lottery." Yet, I noticed that he never actually bought a ticket. It made me skeptical about whether he would ever see the change he desired. The only habit I observed was his tendency to express wishful thinking. Perhaps it made him feel better to say those words, but without taking action, his chances of winning remained impossible.

A different example relates to the fact that this book only exists because of effort expressed in time. More importantly, I didn't begrudge it or feel forced because I wanted to do this more than I wanted to watch YouTube. I felt it was more useful to me based on my values. It's important to establish personal values in relation to time management. For example, I know my life is not an infinite resource and I can't save the world, nor influence the overall universe in any significant way. At best, I can positively influence people to have better lives. Then, hopefully, other people will "pay it forward" and share their knowledge with others to help them learn and grow.

One of my values is to make a positive influence on people. That's where this type of writing fits my value system. It wasn't a daily routine at a specific hour. But it was a priority and I promised myself I'd finish it in a few months. It was on my mind for a couple of years but wasn't "real" until I made a commitment to actually set the time to complete it.

When I was 22, I took a workshop called "More Time." It included tips and a planner book. It was recommended to schedule every 15 minutes of the next day and do only those things you planned in that time slot. It was interesting watching a distraction come along and see if I got hooked on that or not. I found that the 15-minute blocks were too tight for me. I became anxious about my schedule and duties. As suggested, I created those duties the night before. I learned what didn't work for my personality and adjusted to something effective that I liked.

Your scheduling style is your creation and you become your personal slave to the schedule to facilitate a result. It's uncomfortable to look at ourselves sometimes. The tight schedule versus the non-schedule variations forced me to look at the results I wanted versus the progress I wasn't making. I did make adjustments to my work ethic and learned the direct relationship between time, schedule, and results. It's just a basic fact now. Some people say, "Time is Money," implying that time holds monetary value. However, I prefer to say, "Time yields results." This emphasizes that outcomes eventually appear from our use of time. This is similar to changing your mindset from "Practice makes perfect" to "Practice makes progress."

Please take the plunge and try a tight and then a loose schedule to find the balance that produces the results you want and the strictness of being your own slave to it. It won't feel good at times. Sometimes I would tell myself: "Future-Me will look back with appreciation for the work I'm putting in now." I'm being kind to the future me. All true. Very high probability you'll live long enough to enjoy your efforts now and in the years to come.

Push, Pull, and Dodge

Some people I've worked with have called me a machine (as a compliment). They marveled at how much work I got done in a week. I had a trick for being productive and enjoying my life.

Some fun time is necessary to feel good. The key for me is that I put in many more hours on things I valued and very little on meaningless things. Everyone has their own goals and value systems. That was part of the trick; knowing what would be of value to me.

However, when I get low energy I'd need to be creative. That's the other part of the trick. That question nagged me from my late teens: why do I do something that I know isn't good for me? With time, I learned to make agreements with myself. Why do I need to make agreements with myself? It's a conversation that leads to a commitment. It's all discussed: pros and cons etc. In the end, all sides are reviewed. Including situations where I do not have the energy or "I don't feel like it." An example, of a self-agreement, I wouldn't drink enough water. Now 'll put a glass of water where I sit first thing in the morning. It has the implied "do this first" for me. I've already agreed this is good for me and committed to being healthy. It's a reminder process that works.

The Other Part Of the Productivity Trick

I would walk through these next three items when I'm feeling blocked. The techniques are to push, pull or dodge. It works to ask the question and get an answer; clarity by asking a question and listening for the answer. The correct answer is generally the first answer; we need to trust our intuition.

PUSH: Are these activities and goals still in-line with my values? The answer is Yes, No, or Not now. This reminder might be enough to be energized again.

PULL: What will it be like when it's done? What will it feel like if it's not done; ever? I might still not feel like putting effort into it at this time. These questions draw me closer to the goal.

DODGE: Do something else that's a goal/value in a different category (e.g., healthy walking). Do not watch TV or play video games for 4 hours. Dodge is still within a value I have but energizes me as well. This is a choice when Push and Pull aren't working. A change of pace is as good as a rest. A healthy walk is a different priority but still something of value.

Recognizing that nothing can exist without a schedule, it becomes evident that I must dedicate my time to activities aligned with my values if they are to be included in my schedule.

"Procrastination" is basically a distraction we create to avoid completing our goals or schedule. Torturing yourself with "I should" is an interesting distraction that creates internal conflict within ourselves. That's why Dodge works well. It's productive in a different way. It is refreshing because it's something I like to do and has value to me and helps energize me and makes things fresh again.

Value System

Do you actually know what your values are or what you want to achieve? It is important to take time and write these down and implement them into your schedule. A value is something that lasts years or our whole life. It's important to know what you value and put effort only in those lanes. Drifting out of your lane is easy since there are many distractions. Remember progress over perfection.

An effective habit is to time-block in your schedule for people and things that create joy, prosperity, and growth in your life…it is yours to decide. If individuals do not have the same value system as you, then they would be scheduled only as it suits you.

Video Games and Other Vacations

The average number of hours spent on video games is increasing every year. Sure, they're fun, exciting, and have challenges, but rarely do we learn anything that's useful outside the game. Perhaps it may feel too grown-up to quit games and do something "useful". However, in a self-serve universe, we're the only ones that do useful things for ourselves. Mom won't do my laundry forever. That means eventually I'll need to do all those things myself or have the money to hire someone to do them for me. Mom did that because she was raising me from a baby to an adult. But now I have freedom of choice and responsibility for my results. Video games don't have a result but eat an irreplaceable resource: Time.

As an adult, I'll take some time for entertainment. The difference is I have a time budget for non-producing activities. This is me investing and managing my time. Just like I wouldn't put too much money into a bad stock/company, I won't throw away too many hours.

Vacations are great to see and explore, experiencing new places and new things. I've learned "normal" for my country isn't normal for other countries. Obtaining knowledge and a new perspective from vacations is quite interesting. But if I blow all my money on vacations, I'll end up broke by the time I retire. Or worse, I won't have enough money to afford urgent dental care when I need it the most. Not planning for a little bit of savings can be a real pain.

Saving money can grow into a valuable asset through compounding, but saving time can have a similar effect. When I invest some time in learning something new, whether it's through YouTube or other resources, I'm building up my knowledge bank. Even if I don't use that knowledge right away, it may come in handy someday. Plus, exercising my mind and becoming smarter helps not only myself but also the people around me.

I don't set strict schedules for learning because it's something I do regularly. In the same way, I don't tightly plan out my feel-good activities. I go with the flow, but I'm also aware of the consequences of spending too much time on them. I find a balance between enjoying myself and being mindful of how my choices impact my overall well-being.

Your Time: Harnessing the Power of Habits for a Bright Future

Time is one of your most valuable assets; It's like a ticking clock, always moving forward. But here's the cool part: you can make time work for you to build an awesome future that you'll truly enjoy. How? By developing habits that serve you well over time. Let's explore the power of habits and how they can shape your journey to success and happiness.

Time: Your Valuable Asset:
Time is something we can't get back once it's gone. That's why it's crucial to make the most of it. Instead of wasting time on things that don't bring you closer to your goals, imagine using it to create a future filled with exciting possibilities and experiences. Each day is an opportunity to make your time count and take steps toward the life you desire.

The Power of Habits:
Habits are like superpowers that can help you achieve great things. They're the little actions you do consistently, almost without thinking. By creating positive habits, you can make progress over time and build a brighter future. Whether it's studying regularly, exercising, saving money, or practicing a skill, habits shape your life in powerful ways.

For example, let's say you want to become a skilled musician. By dedicating a specific time each day to practice your instrument, you're forming a habit. Over time, this habit will strengthen your skills and bring you closer to your goal of becoming an accomplished musician. With persistence and consistency, your habits will pave the way for success.

Enjoying the Journey:
Building habits isn't just about reaching a distant destination; it's about enjoying the journey along the way. When you create habits that align with your passions and values, you'll find joy in the process of growth and improvement. Each small step you take toward your goals becomes a source of fulfillment, making your journey all the more exciting and rewarding.

Creating Habits That Serve You

To make the most of your time and harness the power of habits, here are a few tips for you:

Set Clear Goals: Identity what you want to achieve in different areas of your life, such as academics, hobbies, relationships, or personal growth. Creating clear goals will guide your habits and keep you focused on what truly matters to you.

Start Small: Remember that habits are built over time, so start with small, manageable actions. For example, if you want to read more, begin by reading a few pages every day. Gradually, you can increase the time and make it a regular habit. Remember…you are seeking progress, not perfection as you go. Trying to be perfect is unsatisfying and unrealistic too.

Stay Consistent: Consistency is key to forming strong habits. Try to perform your chosen habit daily or at regular intervals. Even when you face challenges or setbacks, keep going. The more consistent you are, the more powerful your habits become.

Find Support: Share your goals and habits with supportive friends, family, or mentors. They can provide encouragement and accountability, making it easier for you to stick to your habits and stay motivated. If your current friends aren't supportive, it's time to find some different friends that encourage you to succeed. You can join online groups that are supportive too. The usual caution applies for online groups: some bad actors are in the weeds. Just mute them.

Chapter Summary

Time is a precious asset, and it's up to you to make the most of it. By developing habits that serve you well, you can shape a bright future while enjoying the journey. Embrace the power of habits, set clear goals, start small, stay consistent, and find support along the way. Remember, your time is now. Make it count, and embrace the joy of creating a life you'll love.

3
Emotions and Wealth

Emotions and How They Affect Your Money

Did you know that your feelings can have a big impact on your money? Emotions aren't just about how we feel inside; they can also affect the decisions we make about our finances. Here we'll explore the connection between emotions and wealth and how understanding and managing your emotions can help you make better financial choices.

Emotional Intelligence and Making Money Decisions:
Emotional intelligence is all about understanding and managing your emotions effectively. When it comes to money, being emotionally intelligent can make a big difference in the decisions you make. People with high emotional intelligence are better at making smart choices, resisting impulsive spending, and thinking about the long term. We talked about this earlier in this book.

For example, if you have high emotional intelligence, you'll be less likely to spend all your money on things you want right now. Instead, you'll think about saving and investing for the future. More importantly, when the stock market goes up and down, you won't panic and sell everything because you'll know how to handle your emotions and make rational decisions.

Biases and How They Affect Your Wealth:
We all have biases, which are ways our brains can make mistakes in thinking. These biases can really impact how much money we have. One common bias is called anchoring. It happens when we rely too much on the first piece of information we get and it affects our judgments later on. For example, if you see a stock price that seems really high or really low, you might base your decision on that without considering other important factors.

Another bias that affects wealth is loss aversion. It's when we hate losing something more than we like gaining the same thing. This can make us hold onto investments that are losing money for too long, hoping they'll turn around. But this can stop us from finding better opportunities and growing our wealth.

Behavioral Patterns and Financial Success:
Our emotions can also lead to patterns of behavior that affect how much money we make. For example, if we're scared or anxious, we might avoid taking risks with our money and miss out on good opportunities. On the other hand, if we're too confident and take big risks, we could end up losing most of our money.

Emotional spending is another behavior that can hurt our wealth. Sometimes we buy things to feel better when we're sad or stressed, but this can add up and make it harder to save and invest for the future.

Managing Your Emotions for Financial Success:
Understanding how emotions affect our money can help us manage feelings better and make smarter financial choices. Here are a few tips for doing that:

1. Pay attention to emotions: Notice the feeling when making money decisions. Are you excited, scared, or tempted? Being aware of emotions can help make better choices.

2. Think before spending: Take a moment to think about whether I really need something before buying it. Avoid impulse purchases and save that money for things that truly matter.

3. Get advice from experts: If you're not sure what to do with your money, talk to a financial advisor or someone who knows about money. They can give you good advice and help you make smart decisions, even when emotions are running high.

Emotions have a big impact on wealth. By being aware of personal feelings, understanding biases, and making smart choices, you can improve your financial well-being. Managing your emotion-based actions will set you on a path to financial success and a bright future.

One of the ultimate mental challenges is Day Trading on the stock market. Many day traders I know feel the need to make quick decisions because the market is moving now. However, the most successful day traders keep a journal. Shortly after they make a decision, they record why they bought or sold the stock. This information reveals a pattern that might be completely automatic and invisible to them. This reflective information will allow them to become more knowledgeable about their emotions around winning or losing money

Needless to say, through analysis our spending and buying habits start to become obvious and less painful to review after some time. It's easier to become objective. It's research into higher success. This is the perspective I'd like you to have: being aware of, "What can I do differently or better?" This necessitates a review of facts. You're working on your patterns and that is self-growth.

There was a time in my life when I wanted to become a therapist. Through that journey, I learned something important that I want to share with you. It's highly beneficial to discuss our thoughts and behaviors with someone who is supportive and unbiased. Having a mentor or coach that inspires you to grow is always beneficial. Study the successful people you admire and learn what they did to achieve their success. Let me tell you about two major advantages of doing this.

First, when we open up and talk about our actions, it's a chance to admit them without feeling guilty. By sharing our thoughts and experiences with someone else, we can feel a sense of relief. It's like taking a weight off our shoulders. We don't have to carry everything inside us any more.

Secondly, discussing things with someone objectively gives us a fresh perspective. I had a valuable lesson when someone pointed out something I hadn't considered before. Those "I hadn't thought of that" moments are truly eye-opening and can teach us a lot. So, if you ever find yourself in a situation where you need guidance or want to gain new insights, don't hesitate to seek out someone who can listen to you without judgment. It can make a big difference in your life.

As a habit, I often reflect on what I'm doing and consider if a change is needed. Specifically, I used to mentor day traders for a couple of years, but then I realized something important. There were a few people around me that were day traders and would probably be amazing coaches. It turned out they were much better at teaching than I was. This change came from me reflecting on my own skills and strengths. It's perfectly fine to acknowledge that there are certain things I'm not the absolute best at.

The great thing is that when we recognize our strengths and weaknesses, everyone benefits. It's a win-win situation. By accepting that I'm not the top communicator in that particular area anymore, it has actually freed me up to explore other things. I have the chance to discover new interests and pursue different passions.

Moreover, those new coaches who are truly skilled in mentoring day traders now receive the recognition they deserve. They evolved from day traders to also be coaches. The people being mentored by these new coaches receive the best possible guidance and care.

So, it's all about understanding ourselves, embracing our strengths, and letting go of things that aren't our forte. It opens up exciting opportunities for growth, benefits others around us, and in this case, ensures that those who seek guidance receive the very best support.

Happiness and Pleasure: Understanding the Difference

Let's talk about the difference between happiness and pleasure. To start, we need to understand two important chemicals in our brain: serotonin and dopamine. These chemicals, called neurotransmitters, help transmit signals in our brains. They are automatic. We don't need to tell our brain to do something specific. But our attitudes and the situations we put ourselves in will guide our brain on what to do for us.

Serotonin is all about well-being, regulating our mood, and bringing us a sense of contentment. It helps us feel calm and stable. On the other hand, dopamine is more about pleasure, reward, motivation, and the anticipation of exciting things.

Happiness is all about your mindset, but sometimes life can throw us off balance temporarily. Those fleeting feelings we experience can stick around for an hour or even longer, and if we don't let go of them, they can become part of who we are and how others perceive us.

On the other hand, the pleasure we get from immediate situations doesn't last. That's why people often become addicted to things, actions, or even other people. In simple terms, that excitement we feel when we get new shoes or a new phone only lasts for a short while, maybe a few hours or weeks. It's because our brain releases dopamine, a chemical that reacts to the thrill of something new. This rush is also why some people end up cheating in their relationships.

Flow versus Fireworks: Understanding How Serotonin and Dopamine Affect Our Emotions

Now that we know the basics, let's explore the key differences between these two neurotransmitters. This will be too much detail for some people. It's included here for you.

How the chemical is released:
Serotonin is released steadily and regularly, giving us long-lasting feelings of happiness and contentment. Dopamine, on the other hand, is released in bursts, leading to shorter moments of pleasure and excitement.

What activates the release:
Serotonin is released by activities that make us feel fulfilled and good about ourselves, like acts of kindness, social connections, and self-care. Dopamine, however, is triggered by new and thrilling experiences, unexpected rewards, and exciting situations.

Effect on Mood:
Serotonin helps stabilize our mood and emotional balance, giving us an overall sense of happiness and peace. Dopamine can create intense highs and lows, and sometimes even lead to addictive behaviors, although it can also bring positive emotions.

Is it addictive:
Serotonin is not directly associated with addiction. It focuses more on emotional stability and contentment. Dopamine, on the other hand, plays a big role in the brain's reward pathway and can drive addictive behaviors when it's excessively activated.

What lasts longer:
Serotonin's effects last longer, contributing to sustained happiness and well-being. Dopamine's effects, on the other hand, are shorter-lived, often leaving us wanting more pleasure and excitement.

Mental health:
Having a healthy balance of serotonin is crucial for our overall well-being and mental health. It helps regulate our mood, sleep, and appetite. Dopamine, while important for motivation and rewards, needs to be balanced to prevent impulsive behavior and excessive seeking of pleasure.

Happiness:
Serotonin plays a vital role in long-term happiness and life satisfaction. It focuses on contentment and emotional stability. Dopamine, with its association with pleasure and reward, adds moments of excitement and enjoyment to our lives, but it doesn't guarantee lasting happiness.

While pleasure and happiness are both important, they come from different places in our brain. Grasping these differences can help us make choices that lead to a more balanced and fulfilling life.

The Dark Side of Dopamine

Exploring Dopamine Detox and Addiction: What You Need to Know.

Let's break down the concept of dopamine detox and how it relates to addiction in a way that makes sense for non-medical readers. Dopamine detox is basically taking a break from activities that give our brain a big rush of dopamine. You know that awesome feeling you get when you do something fun or exciting? Well, that's dopamine in action. But sometimes we can get carried away and overdo it.

Imagine you're playing video games for hours on end or scrolling through social media endlessly. These activities can flood your brain with dopamine, and while it feels great in the moment, it can also mess with your brain's reward system. That's where dopamine detox comes in. It's about intentionally stepping back and giving your brain a break from those super-rewarding activities.

Dr. Anna Lembke, an expert in the science of addiction, has talked about how dopamine plays a role in addiction. As mentioned earlier, dopamine is a chemical in your brain that gets released when you do something enjoyable or rewarding. It's like a pat on the back for your brain saying, "Hey, that was awesome let's do it again!" But when certain substances or behaviors constantly trigger dopamine release which can lead to a cycle of craving and compulsive use, this is what happens in addiction.

Understanding how addiction works means delving into the science of your brain's reward system. It's about figuring out how drugs or certain behaviors can take over and make you feel like you need them all the time. Dr. Anna Lembke, being an expert in this field, has some cool insights into how addiction affects our brains and what we can do about it.

By learning about dopamine detox and the neuroscience of addiction, you can gain a better understanding of how your brain works and the potential risks of overindulging in certain activities. It's all about finding a healthy balance and making choices that support your well-being.

I attended a seminar with Tav Sparks, an ex-addict turned world-class advisor. He would try anything to get a high, "Anything!" in his own words. For him, it took breathwork and other physical and mental processes to take control of his life again. This was not "fun". This is the dark side of the rush and constantly needing another. If you can limit the desire for the rush, you won't have to claw back from the dark side, and not be trapped there. If there is a hell on Earth, I'm sure addiction would be part of it.

Being Bored: Unleash Your Superpower!

Did you know that being bored can actually be a superpower? Instead of feeling restless or uninterested, being bored can be an opportunity for discovery. It's a chance to explore and find your passion or even a way to improve your income. So, instead of sticking to the same routine every day in search of happiness, why not venture out and explore the unknown?

Think about it: your new favorite place is somewhere you haven't been yet. By embracing boredom and stepping out of your comfort zone, you open yourself up to exciting possibilities. It's like unlocking a door to a world full of new experiences, hobbies, and interests.

Next time you find yourself feeling bored, take a moment to look around and see what catches your attention. What piques your curiosity? Is there something you've always wanted to try but never had the chance? Use this downtime to delve into new activities, explore different subjects, or even learn a new skill. You might discover a hidden talent or a passion you never knew existed!

Don't limit yourself to what you already know. Expand your horizons and seek out fresh experiences. Whether it's trying out a new sport, visiting a place you've never been to, or even experimenting with creative projects, the possibilities are endless.

In studies of younger people, they often go to their cellphones to watch content whenever they have idle moments. This adds to general awareness but doesn't contribute to their goals. I'm suggesting putting something else on the phone (such as a goal sheet and things that deserve our attention). You'd be surprised the impact to your life by this one change.

Chapter Summary

Start looking around for what your passion is, perhaps this may create additional income. Embrace it as an invitation to seek out new adventures, cultivate your interests, and uncover hidden talents. The next time you're feeling bored, see it as an exciting opportunity to embark on a journey of self-discovery. Who knows what amazing things you'll find along the way?

4
Empowering Yourself in a Complicated World

Navigating the Complexities

Sometimes, people tend to complicate things unnecessarily. I'm not a medical expert, so I won't give you medical advice. But if I have a headache, I'll often take a pill for it. What I want to say is that sometimes it's important to hire professionals, while other times it's good to have a basic understanding of what they're doing for you. You have to determine whether or not seeking the help of an expert works for you.

Personally, I've taken the initiative to learn about topics like law and psychology that apply to all of us. The law is all around us, and although some laws may seem confusing, they often have hidden reasons behind them. The legal system is complex and requires experts at times.

I strongly believe in things like respecting others and not causing harm, which is why I appreciate laws. While laws can't physically stop a bullet, they can deter violence to some extent. That's all I ask for. I won't harm others, and I hope others won't harm me. Thanks to laws and the people who enforce them, I generally feel safe. Learning legal principles was helpful to me at times but ultimately wasn't a career path I followed. It gave me some useful insights into what the law can do and what it did not do for individuals. Essentially, the laws reflect the bigger scope called society. It defines the boundaries for us. And if something gets complicated, I get legal help from a professional.

Psychology helps us understand where people break smaller, personal boundaries. Understanding psychology is valuable on a day-to-day basis because it helps us grasp the basic motivations that drive people, including ourselves. From my observation, about 30% of people genuinely care about others, while the majority may casually litter the sides of roads, expecting someone else to clean up after them. They also know that they are unlikely to be caught by the law. ["It's not littering unless I get caught."] This is just a reality we have to accept. That's why it's important to learn some basic psychology about human behavior. Be prepared for the fact that some people will lie to get your money. This is where knowing the basics of law and psychology is helpful.

Speaking from personal experience, I've trusted too many people too easily in the past. If I had known more about people and their underlying motivations, I would have saved a lot of money and heartache! Even intelligent individuals can fall victim to scams. Just look at the case of Bernie Madoff, where industry experts were convinced that Madoff Investments was a safe place to invest their money.

When it comes to investments, things can get complicated. The advice comes from all directions, each claiming to have the right answer. I used to trust some of those investment professionals who worked for a popular and well-established institution when my family was young. However, the fine print allowed them to lose most of my money without any consequences. How did that help me? It didn't. It only helped the investment salesperson and their superiors earn a commission. Needless to say, these "professionals" didn't have my best interest at heart.

So, I decided to prioritize learning more about money and basic investing. I even obtained a Securities License and took on a part-time job at a small investment company. Surprisingly, this allowed me to promote both the good and the bad investments. The manager decided which ones to promote to clients. What I discovered was that the general investment advice offered produced mediocre results. After just one month, I quit my part-time job because I realized there's more to investing than what meets the eye. But that's a story for another time. I had the basic information which was not readily available online but now is available along with misinformation too.

Here I was, armed with some knowledge about the complex investment industry, yet still unsure of how to distinguish between good and bad investments. Passing the exam for the Securities License meant I understood the basic tools, but it didn't teach good investing.

It turns out that individuals like Madoff and the Enron scandal lied about the assets within their investments. They made their investments look good on paper. This deception is similar to the stories of sales agents but on a deeper level. After years of research, I finally found a few reliable approaches that can't contain any lies. These strategies yield better results than the mediocre ones those salespeople often promote. And the best part is that there are little to no commissions involved, which means more money for your retirement, not theirs.

Putting all this together, Bernie Madoff used psychology and intelligence to skirt the law for many years. He promoted a bad investment to savvy professionals. They were experts and got fooled because they didn't look any deeper. They trusted the numbers on paper. They trusted Bernie too much and he made-off with their billions. This is a risk of putting too much energy and money into a single place.

I'll get to better investing ideas later in this book. But before that, let's see if you can recognize Madoff-like presenters.

Unmasking "Tipsters"

Here is a summary of a book based on the history of advice-givers and people's willingness to take bad advice. The advice-givers were called "Tipsters"; giving tips that might not be vetted or contrary to the listeners' best interest. The listener gladly received the advice in the hopes of a profitable advantage. And if the advice turned out badly, they wouldn't blame the giver because it was freely given on the hush-hush. The listener would often go back to the tipster for the next great hot tip.

Introduction:
In the book "Reminiscences of a Stock Operator" written by Edwin LeFevre, we are taken on a trip into the intriguing world of stock trading and learn valuable lessons about the role of tipsters and people's willingness to follow their advice. This summary aims to shed light on the dangers and pitfalls of blindly trusting tipsters.

The Temptation of Tipsters:

In the stock market, tipsters are individuals who claim to have insider information or secret strategies that can help you make a fortune. They often appear confident and persuasive, enticing people to follow their recommendations. However, it's important to approach their advice with caution.

The Illusion of Expertise:

Tipsters present themselves as experts in the field, creating an illusion of knowledge and success. They might boast about their past predictions or use fancy jargon to impress their audience. But remember, true expertise is built on experience, research, and a deep understanding of the market, not just empty promises.

The Hidden Motives:

Behind the mask of helpfulness, tipsters often have hidden motives. They may stand to gain financially by convincing others to buy or sell certain stocks. It's essential to question their intentions and consider whether their advice aligns with your own financial goals and interests.

The Bandwagon Effect:

One reason people fall for tipsters is the bandwagon effect. When we see others following a tipster's advice and seemingly making money, we feel compelled to join in, fearing that we might miss out on the next big opportunity. However, it's crucial to remember that markets are unpredictable, and blindly following the crowd can lead to costly mistakes.

The Dangers of Rumors:

Tipsters often rely on rumors and hearsay to fuel their recommendations. They may spread false information or exaggerate certain events to manipulate stock prices in their favor. It's vital to verify information from reliable sources before making any investment decisions.

The Importance of Due Diligence:

Instead of relying solely on tipsters, young adults should embrace the concept of due diligence. This involves conducting thorough research, analyzing market trends, and understanding the fundamentals of the companies they want to invest in. By empowering themselves with knowledge, they can make informed decisions and become more independent investors.

Learning from Mistakes:
One of the key takeaways from "Reminiscences of a Stock Operator" is the importance of learning from mistakes. Even experienced investors make errors, but what sets them apart is their ability to reflect on their actions, adapt their strategies, and continuously improve. Embrace the learning process and use setbacks as opportunities for growth.

Key Takeaways:
While tipsters may seem enticing, young adults must approach their advice with skepticism. The stock market is complex and unpredictable, requiring diligent research and careful decision-making. By learning from the lessons shared in "Reminiscences of a Stock Operator," we can become more discerning investors, relying on verifiable or personal knowledge and analysis rather than blindly following the advice of others.
Although that book was written 100 years ago and was based on experiences spanning 50 years before it, human behavior is still relevant today and tomorrow.
Reminiscences of a Stock Operator - Wikipedia

Unmasking Modern Tipsters - Their Rivers of Belief

In the exciting world of finance, it's important for us to navigate wisely and avoid falling for deceptive practices. Let's delve into common pitfalls, offering valuable insights to empower us to make financial decisions.

The Deceptive TV Show Host:
Imagine an exuberant TV show host who appears to have all the answers. However, it's crucial to look beyond their charismatic presentation. If you dig into their past, you might uncover reasons not to fully trust them. Also, you can track the results of their recommendations on platforms like Reddit, and you'll discover that their actual performance isn't as thrilling as their energetic persona suggests. There are simple, less flashy strategies that may consistently outperform their recommendations.

The Newsletter Phenomenon:
Since the 1950s, newsletters promoting stock picks have flooded the market. They often highlight their best-performing picks to attract subscribers. But here's the catch: they rarely share their average returns, which provide a more accurate measure of their overall performance. By cataloging numerous publications, and looking beyond attention-grabbing titles, you can gain a clearer understanding of a newsletter's true value before investing any money. I kept many published newsletters for later review and for some I actually had a subscription. You should know that some have been successfully sued for front-running their recommendations and making millions from them. They didn't disclose that they owned those stocks before pumping them.

The Challenge of Outperforming the Market:
It's important to remember that consistently beating the overall market average is extremely difficult. While a few individuals have achieved this feat, they are exceptions rather than the norm. Even professional investors and analysts struggle to consistently outpace the market. This is because stock prices incorporate all available information, making it hard to consistently find undervalued or overvalued stocks. Understanding this reality helps us set realistic expectations and approach our investments with a long-term perspective.

Wrap-up:
Mega-trends are an easier strategy. For example, cell phones. In the beginning, the share price of those companies was shaky but in the long term turned out very well.

By arming yourself with knowledge and awareness, you can become a savvy investor who sees through deceptive financial practices. You can make informed decisions, avoiding the pitfalls of blindly following charismatic personalities or trusting selective reporting. With a little caution, you can increase your chances of making sound financial choices and achieving long-term success in the complex world of finance.

Megatrends and Investing: Unlocking Opportunities

In the dynamic world of investing, understanding megatrends can be a powerful tool for making informed financial decisions. This section aims to shed light on the concept of megatrends and how they can shape investment opportunities, empowering would-be investors to navigate the ever-changing investment landscape. The core concept of a megatrend is something that is unstoppable demand by consumers. That's why it's a good strategy. But it doesn't mean every company will be a success in that emerging area; as we'll find out in the next section.

What are Megatrends?
Megatrends are long-term, transformative forces that have the potential to significantly impact various aspects of society, the economy, and our daily lives. They arise from global shifts in demographics, technology, social dynamics, and environmental factors. Examples of megatrends include the rise in renewable energy, the growth of the digital economy, shifts in consumer behavior, and advancements in healthcare technology.

Recognizing Megatrends:
To identify megatrends, investors can pay attention to societal changes, emerging technologies, and global challenges. Megatrends often reflect shifts in values, preferences, and the needs of an evolving world. Keeping a finger on the pulse of these trends can provide

insights into potential investment opportunities that align with the changing landscape.

Investment Opportunities:
Megatrends present investors with exciting opportunities to align their investments with the forces shaping the future. For instance, renewable energy is a megatrend driven by the growing concern for sustainability and climate change. Investing in companies involved in clean energy solutions or supporting the development of renewable technologies can be both financially rewarding and socially impactful.

Diversification and Long-Term Perspective:
To effectively invest in megatrends, it is important for investors to diversify their portfolios because even a frontrunner in a particular field can experience setbacks along the way. Megatrends can extend over several years or even decades, so it is crucial to maintain patience and adopt a long-term perspective. By diversifying across different sectors and asset classes, investors can reduce risks and seize potential returns from a range of megatrends. It's helpful to learn about the S-Curve pattern of technological innovation and adoption.

Conducting Research and Due Diligence:
Before investing in specific megatrends, investors should conduct thorough research and due diligence. This includes analyzing market trends, assessing the potential risks and rewards, and considering the expertise and track record of companies within the chosen megatrend. Staying informed and seeking guidance from financial professionals can help make well-informed investment decisions. It is important to be ready to make changes when significant changes happen for the trend or a company.

Key Takeaways:
Understanding megatrends and their potential impact on the world can empower us to identify investment opportunities that align with our values and long-term goals. By recognizing the transformative forces shaping society and investing with a diversified portfolio, investors can participate in the growth of innovative industries and contribute to a sustainable future. Remember, staying informed, conducting research,

and seeking guidance are the keys to navigating the exciting world of megatrends and unlocking investment opportunities.

Which horse will win the megatrend race?

In the fast-paced world of technology, the story of Nokia and Apple serves as a striking example of how those companies can experience dramatically different outcomes within the same megatrend. Both companies entered the mobile phone market, but while Apple thrived and revolutionized the industry, Nokia struggled and ultimately failed. The primary reason for Nokia's downfall was its inability to adapt and stay ahead of the evolving landscape.

Nokia, once a dominant player in the mobile phone market, enjoyed widespread popularity with its innovative devices. However, as the megatrend of smartphones emerged, Nokia failed to anticipate and embrace the shift towards touchscreen technology, app ecosystems, and enhanced user experiences. Meanwhile, Apple recognized the changing consumer preferences and released the revolutionary iPhone, captivating users with its sleek design, intuitive interface, and robust ecosystem of applications. Blackberry was technically the first smartphone, but we'll leave them aside for this discussion.

While Nokia remained committed to its traditional feature phones and resisted embracing the smartphone revolution, Apple seized the opportunity to redefine the mobile industry. The iPhone's seamless integration of hardware and software, combined with its user-friendly interface and innovative features, captured the hearts of consumers worldwide. Apple's ability to adapt and embrace the megatrend propelled them to unparalleled success, while Nokia struggled to keep up with the changing demands of the market. As Steve Jobs implied, users don't know what they want until they see it or hold it. He was a visionary leader.

The Nokia-Apple comparison highlights the importance of adaptability and forward-thinking in the face of megatrends. It serves as a reminder that even companies with established market presence can falter if they fail to recognize and respond to shifting industry dynamics. The ability to pivot, innovate, and continuously meet evolving consumer needs is crucial for long-term success within a megatrend.

The story of Nokia and Apple serves as a valuable lesson for young adults entering the business world. This emphasizes the importance of being open to change, embracing new technologies, and constantly seeking ways to innovate and stay ahead of the curve. By understanding the significance of adaptation within megatrends, entrepreneurs and aspiring business leaders can position themselves for success and avoid the pitfalls of complacency. Flexibility, agility, and a willingness to embrace change are key attributes that can make a significant difference in thriving within megatrends and shaping the future of industries.

Flexibility Beats Old Knowledge

Intelligence isn't as valuable as flexibility. For example, a recent job classification that has gone mostly obsolete is that of a film projectionist. In the past, when movies were predominantly shown on 35mm film reels in theaters, film projectionists played a crucial role in operating the projectors and ensuring a seamless movie-watching experience for audiences. They were responsible for loading film reels, adjusting the projection speed, and ensuring proper focus and sound synchronization.

However, with the advent of digital cinema technology and the widespread adoption of digital projectors, the need for film projectionists has disappeared with it. Digital cinema eliminates the need for physical film prints and the manual operation of projectors. This transition has streamlined the projection process, making it more efficient and cost-effective for theater owners. The cost was a key driver for business owners, as it always motivates for-profit companies.

As a result, the role of film projectionist has become increasingly rare. The skills once required to handle film reels and operate complex projection equipment are no longer in demand. The advancement of technology has transformed the cinema industry and reshaped the job market.

Not popular means no-market. When the NASA space program (trips to the moon) shut down in the 70s many very intelligent, skilled people went out of work. The movie "Hidden Figures" highlights the women (called computers) that did the calculations for NASA. They were replaced by electronic computers, subsequently, some of these individuals adapted and became computer programmers.

A book published in 1859 by Charles Darwin was one of the first to talk about the concept of "Adapt or Die." This idea applies not only to living organisms but also to companies and employees. A great example of this can be seen in the movie "Moneyball." The key to success is being flexible and adaptable. Ask any dinosaur.

Chapter Summary

In a world characterized by constant change and complexity, the ability to be flexible and adaptable is crucial to success in various contexts. Whether it's personal decision-making, navigating financial markets, or thriving within megatrends, by responding to shifting circumstances and embracing new technologies with an open and adaptable mind that welcomes change, you position yourself to seize opportunities for growth and stay ahead of the curve in an ever-changing landscape. More importantly, many tools can alert you to changes making it easier to be agile.

5
Careers and the Best You

You're well-suited for the new normal. Children who grew up in a world with smartphones learned to type with their thumbs. Older people generally poke at the screen with one finger because smartphones weren't their "normal" growing up. Their normal was having a phone connected to a wall. They possess skills that may seem outdated to you, like using a rotary dial. On the other hand, you have skills that you take for granted, skills that older generations don't and won't have.

Competition

Are you ready to make your mark and stand out from the crowd? In the past, people could rely on being smart and finding good jobs, but times have changed. Nowadays, millions of people are interconnected and competing for the same online jobs. It gets even more challenging when you consider that artificial intelligence is also vying for these jobs, and there seems to be an endless stream of new artificially intelligent ("AI") devices emerging all the time.

In an ideal scenario, if you're in a job that requires intelligence, you would use artificial intelligence to assist you rather than replace you completely. We're now in an era where we embrace the help of AI, recognizing it as a tool that complements our abilities. However, when it comes to physical jobs, robots are taking over tasks that were traditionally done by humans. This isn't a new trend; it has been happening for many years. In areas like manufacturing and warehousing, mechanical devices have often replaced jobs, improving safety for everyone involved. It is important to remember that technological advancement is here to stay. This means we need to individually adapt to changes because the rate of change is accelerating.

AI Doesn't Have Dreams

The most common threat young adults see is AI taking away jobs. I have extensive experience with artificial intelligence and creating automated trading algorithms for financial markets. Having worked with computers since I was 13, I'm quite familiar with this topic. In recent years, many people have heard about AI, but they often don't fully understand how it works or its limitations. Some people even feel a bit scared because they don't know the limits of this powerful intruder. However, one of my friends views it all as pure magic.

When I was young, I thought there was no point in becoming a computer programmer because computers would eventually become smart enough to program themselves. However, I pursued a career as a software developer anyway because there were plenty of well-paying job opportunities.

Many years ago I read the book "The Art of War." I learned a valuable principle that has been incredibly useful to me in changing conditions. To put it in my own words, the lesson I took away was to 'attack where your enemy cannot or will not defend.' Applying this to artificial intelligence means identifying the areas where it can't or won't replace me. We possess dreams, visions, and the ability to be inspired by things that artificial intelligence cannot create. AI lacks pure creativity. It can take existing knowledge and generate modified versions based on your instructions, combining different elements to create something new. While computers excel at mathematical processes and can achieve incredible feats with AI, they won't create an entirely new music genre, for instance.

Here's my summary of AI. Similar to what is said about fire: It is a good servant (providing warmth for your home) but a terrible master (burning your house down). Basically don't let fire get out of the fireplace. I think the same can be said about AI. Don't let AI be in control of humans. Some groups are working with the government to establish regulations in this regard. This means that AI is likely to play a supportive role in your life, but it's crucial not to let it take control.

For a deeper dive into AI and Humans, you could get the book "Artificial Intelligence: A guide for Thinking Humans" by Melanie Mitchell.

What Career Advice Do You Have?

Well, I can't give you specific advice, but I can point you in the right direction. There are plenty of resources available to help you figure out what career path might be right for you. One helpful tool is called the Enneagram, which is a system that categorizes people into nine basic types based on their personality traits. It can give you some insight into what kind of work might suit you best. For example, do you prefer repetitive tasks like a bookkeeper, or do you thrive on face-to-face interactions with people? Answering questions like these can be a good starting point.

If you're not sure where to begin, try brainstorming topics that you're interested in. Write them down in bubbles on a piece of paper or use mind-map tools to visualize your ideas. As you start jotting down your interests, you'll find that more topics come to mind. This process of emptying your thoughts onto paper can be really helpful.

Once you have around 20 bubbles, start connecting them with lines. This will help you see connections between different topics and discover something that is uniquely you. Sometimes, you might come across unusual and specific career paths that surprise you. For example, you might hear about a study on nighttime beetle movements in a jungle and wonder who would ever be interested in that. But some people are passionate about such things and even get funding to conduct full studies. Could you be one of those people?

Remember, sometimes great careers can come from unexpected places. Steve Jobs, the co-founder of Apple, stumbled upon calligraphy while in school. It wasn't something he had planned, but he enjoyed it. Now, we have a wide variety of fonts on websites and phones, all thanks to his interest in calligraphy. So, imagine the bubbles and lines that could have been on his brainstorming sheet that led him to such groundbreaking innovations.

What Would Shannon Do?

Throughout history, there have been countless brilliant minds who have left their mark. Think of people like Leonardo da Vinci, Johann Bach, Albert Einstein, and Claude Shannon. But imagine if they were born in our era. They wouldn't simply replicate what they had done before; instead, they would create something entirely new, relevant to today's world. They might take inspiration from their predecessors and build upon their work or uncover fresh opportunities in our modern society.

When it comes to choosing your own path, you have two options: you can follow in the footsteps of those who came before you, or you can venture into uncharted territory. The latter may seem more challenging, but it's just a different path to invest your time in, rather than pursuing a conventional career.

Imagine two ships departing from a harbor, each set sail on a slightly different course. At first, the difference between them may appear insignificant. However, as time passes, they end up in vastly different destinations based on their respective routes. Careers work similarly. A slight shift in direction can lead to significant differences in where you end up as time marches on. The calendar moves forward relentlessly, without waiting for anyone. It's automated, ticking away with each passing moment. The question is, how will you make use of this automated passage of time? I tried a few careers until I settled on one as primary.

You can be snug in a job that might not change for many years, or take a risky exploration. Neither path is easy and they both have costs. Your path fits your personality. Ignore the critics since it's your life in this self-serve universe. You feed yourself. All the decisions are yours and there will be random events that may change your career entirely. If you're breathing, you have choices and might as well do something.

Life is like an empty canvas, waiting for us to pick up our brushes and paint upon it, creating our unique masterpiece. Paint over the parts you don't like anymore. You possess the power to shape your own narrative. Use your sparks of inspiration that ignite your soul. We all make mistakes. That's truly an unavoidable part of being alive. Lessons will be repeated until we actually learn from them.

If you are having doubts someday, imagine the words of passionate motivational speakers echoing in your ears: "Channel your inner brilliance and unleash your potential upon the world. With every stroke of creativity and every purposeful step, you infuse the tapestry of existence with vibrant colors. Embrace the limitless possibilities that lay ahead, for within your grasp lies the chance to craft a masterpiece uniquely your own."

My personality is more conservative. So I don't speak like that. Pick a voice that serves you. You can change that voice whenever you like. You can use a virtual guide too: What would Claude Shannon do? I had a negative parent's voice in my head for far too long. I purged that and am happier. Do what you need to look after your internal and external states.

Self-Validation

In today's world, where social media plays a significant role in our lives, it's important to recognize the power of self-validation. Let's think about the idea of needing validation from others, like seeking approval through likes on a post. When we constantly rely on this external feedback, it can indicate that we are not fully in control of our own lives. It's like we're giving others the power to determine our self-worth based on shallow judgments.

But here's the thing: true fulfillment and happiness come from within. When we learn to validate ourselves, we free ourselves from the addictive cycle of seeking constant validation on social media. Instead, we become self-directed individuals who define our paths and value ourselves based on our standards.

Numerous studies have shed light on the negative effects of excessive social media use, especially among young people. It can lead to decreased self-esteem, increased anxiety, and even feelings of isolation. However, by shifting our focus inward and embracing self-validation, we can break free from these harmful patterns.

So, how can we practice self-validation? It starts with recognizing our own accomplishments, strengths, and unique qualities. We need to celebrate our successes, both big and small, without needing the approval of others. It's about acknowledging our worthiness and embracing self-love.

By cultivating self-validation, we empower ourselves to make choices that align with our authentic selves. We become less affected by the superficial judgments of others and more in tune with our passions, goals, and values. So, let's remember that the true power lies within us, and by relying on self-validation instead of social media validation, we can pave the way for a more fulfilling and self-directed life.

The Power of Declarations

We humans possess an incredible ability to alter our thinking patterns. The speed at which we learn as individuals can vary greatly depending on the learning style we adopt.

First, let's look at using our internal system to help us. How can we hack our brains?

Our brain operates through numerous sub-processes, each often functioning independently from the others. Interestingly, it has been found that the reason we naturally engage in self-talk, speaking out loud to ourselves, is to facilitate the collaboration of these separate processes. By doing so, we can align them towards a common purpose. This alignment is essential and necessary for optimal functioning.

Second, I feel that declarations are very powerful. When the United States wanted to become its own country, it declared its independence. Similarly, when we speak to ourselves, we often make declarations. Let's break down the word "declare": "De" means "of" or "from," and "clare" means "clarity." So, "de-clare" means expressing something that comes from clarity. It's like when we discover something new, express it, and firmly support it.

Every human makes declarations every day, whether we realize it or not. Some are repetitive sound bites from our parents, while others are new thoughts we have. About 99% of what we tell ourselves today will probably be on tomorrow's list too. It's like a never-ending background loop. But we have the power to change that.

Negative perspectives from our parents or other people around us can influence our background thoughts. It's important to clean out those negative thoughts from our minds, just like house cleaning. Cleaning creates space to be a renewed self. We have both positive and negative thoughts playing in our heads, and the good news is that we can change them. It might take some time to recognize them at first, but the first step is to give them a name. Why do I always have a certain mood or perspective? It's all buried in our daily thought process. When I was younger, I used to wonder why some people were more cheerful than me. I didn't understand it back then.

Our inner dialogue is incredibly powerful and has a big impact on our future. It influences the decisions we make and shapes our thoughts. Our thoughts are like liquid, and our inner dialogue acts as the bottle that contains them. Thoughts that don't fit the bottle are automatically dismissed without even realizing it. We don't get to explore those ideas further. Some people might read this and not fully grasp what I'm saying, and that's okay. Our brains have mechanisms to filter out ideas. These mechanisms are there to protect us from distractions. Their job is to quickly dismiss things that sound stupid or off-topic. That's why a few readers will need to re-read this paragraph slowly.

For instance, imagine someone telling me they believe the moon is made of cheese. I explain that we've sent people to the moon, brought back samples, and conducted tests, so it's not entirely made of cheese. Yet, they still insist it is. No matter what facts or logical arguments I present, they won't budge. In such cases, it's not worth my time trying to convince someone who won't listen to reason.

As an experiment, try listening to your body for 10 seconds and notice how you feel energetically. Now, tell yourself, "I'm 90 years old." How do you feel in your body now? Repeat the experiment by telling yourself, "I'm 10. I'm young." Did your energy level change? For most people, their feelings change based on the words they tell themselves. It may seem like just words, but our bodies listen and respond to those thoughts. Thoughts have the power to create our feelings!

This brings us back to declarations. We say things to ourselves all day long, and those are our declarations. You can also think of them as assertions if you prefer. That's why it's crucial to edit our inner narrative. I know someone who constantly tells themselves, "I never get sick," and surprisingly, they rarely get sick. Is it just a coincidence or is there a cause-and-effect relationship? Are they ignoring reality or actually influencing their immune system?

Once, while attending a workshop, I witnessed someone being told they were really smart. The listener was taken aback and couldn't believe it. As they engaged in a conversation to explore this further, they realized they had a negative narrative about themselves that they had formed when they were younger. They were not even aware of the narrative. It's just always there and a "normal" conclusion was made a long time ago. It's just a fact in their mind. When they were confronted with facts that didn't fit their negative narrative…something had to change. Eventually, with practice, they were able to change the negative feedback loop in their brain and believe they were intelligent. That's just how our brains are wired and it tries to help and protect us, but it's up to us to break free from our old ways of negative thinking.

Guided Declarations

I've shared a guide with a few people on how to make powerful and uplifting declarations that actually work and make you feel good. You see, there are many people out there talking about affirmations, like saying "I'm a millionaire." But here's the thing: our brain knows the truth, and it won't easily accept something that isn't aligned with our current reality. If you're *not* already what the affirmation claims, it won't work for you. It might even work against you, causing frustration.

A better approach is to use statements like "I'm becoming" or "I'm studying" or "I choose to be," something that you desire. These statements reflect the truth and reaffirm your goals. They acknowledge the qualities you already possess and the skills you want to develop. Know what you want to achieve and then create a positive inner dialogue just for yourself.

Here's an activity you can try: Write down some good qualities that others have complimented you on. There are neurological reasons for using a pen and paper. Include the desires you wish to achieve as well. Then, find a place where you can put these words, somewhere that's personal and private, like the back of your bedroom door. It's a subtle reminder that only you know about, but it will catch your attention every time you walk past it. These words become part of your background thoughts, working in your subconscious mind. Another suggestion is to create your passwords about your dreams or future goals, for example, learn$1000Perday, IloveGreece, Healthinspired...what are yours?

Remember, your subconscious mind is always active, so feed it the right thoughts and direction. By doing this, you're using your conscious thoughts and actions to steer your automatic, unconscious processes in a positive direction that benefits you.

Here's an alternate approach that I did and worked very well for me. It's a different style of declaration. I made a list of the traits I admire in other people. Easy enough to come up with that. Probably one of the best hours I've spent in my life for its positive effect on me. Then I framed a new me as that person. I envisioned myself being that way; with those traits I admired. I thought of it as "becoming the person I admire".

So go ahead and give some of this a try! Take control of your background thoughts and use them to empower yourself.

Taking a Career You Don't Like: Health Effects and Examples

In Chapter 2 we looked at the 3 assets you have. One of them is your health.

Choosing a career that you don't enjoy can have significant impacts on your health and well-being. When you're stuck in a job that doesn't fulfill you, it can lead to increased stress, anxiety, and even physical health problems. Imagine spending most of your waking hours doing something that doesn't bring you joy or satisfaction. The constant stress and dissatisfaction can take a toll on your mental and emotional health, affecting your overall quality of life.

Some well-known examples of this can be seen in the stories of individuals who pursued careers they didn't love. Take Steve Jobs, the co-founder of Apple Inc., as an example. In his early years, Jobs worked in a field he didn't enjoy and later described it as a period of disappointment and frustration. However, when he followed his passion for technology and design, he became one of the most successful and influential figures in the tech industry. His story highlights the negative effects of being in a career you don't like and the transformative power of pursuing what you love.

Sometimes, when I go to a store I can easily tell who loves their job or is simply slogging through their day. Negative energy at work builds a mood that gets brought home. Month after month that affects the immune system and creates mental anxiety. If you're in a job to pay the bills, it can be done with a goal in mind that's positive. Abraham Lincoln endured being president during the worst time in their history. His thoughts: "And this too will change."

Choosing a Career You Love: Health Benefits and Examples

Selecting a career that aligns with your passions and interests can have numerous positive effects on your health and well-being. When you wake up excited about your work, it boosts your overall happiness and a sense of fulfillment. Studies have shown that individuals who are engaged and passionate about their jobs tend to experience lower levels of stress and have improved mental health. They often have higher job satisfaction, which can translate into better physical health as well. A well-known example is Oprah Winfrey, a prominent media personality. Winfrey's career began as a news anchor, but she soon discovered her passion for hosting talk shows. By pursuing her love for communication and storytelling, she became an influential media mogul and philanthropist (and a billionaire). Her inspiring journey exemplifies the positive impact that pursuing a career you love can have on both your professional success and overall well-being.

Imagine waking up each morning excited to go to work because you're pursuing your passion. Research suggests that being engaged in a career you love can have numerous health benefits. When you're passionate about your work, you're more likely to experience job satisfaction, reduced stress levels, and improved mental well-being. Take the example of Serena Williams, one of the greatest tennis players of all time. Serena's passion for tennis led her to a highly successful career. Her dedication, love for the sport, and the joy she derives from playing have not only brought her recognition but also positively impacted her mental and physical health. She serves as an inspiration, showing that pursuing a career you love can contribute to overall well-being.

The career path you choose can have profound effects on your health. Opting for a job that you don't enjoy can lead to increased stress and dissatisfaction, negatively impacting your mental and emotional well-being. Conversely, pursuing a career that you love can bring joy, fulfillment, and improved mental health. Examples like Steve Jobs, Oprah Winfrey, and Serena Williams demonstrate the stark contrast between the negative consequences of a disliked career and the transformative power of following your passion. It's essential to prioritize your happiness and well-being when making career choices, as they can significantly shape your overall quality of life.

Getting Maximum Value from Books

Since you've made it this far, I want to tell you about how I read a book to get the most value from it. I noticed when I read something that I'd forget about the majority of the details within a week. As time progressed I'd forget everything but a key principle. So I started reading books differently to get the value it offers. If I liked what was being said and there was a useful tip in the book, I'd put the book down and implement what I could to get the maximum value. Here I'm suggesting you go back to parts that you thought could be useful for you to have. Make notes or whatever you need to do, but put this book away until some action is performed. Something that will work for you in the future. For example:

- List your values as they might drive the career you choose.
- What habits do you need to make or change?
- Did you set a time to learn more about megatrends (like put that on your calendar for next week)?
- Make a declaration sheet.

These are ideas for your growth; for the best you possible. Growth leads to more freedom.

Chapter Summary

The choices you make about your career can shape your health and happiness. It's essential to find a balance between pursuing your passions and considering practical aspects. When you follow your interests, skills, and values, you increase the chances of finding a fulfilling career that brings you joy and contributes to a healthier, more satisfying life.

In short, don't take a job you hate unless you're desperate for food or rent. And then start searching for something better…don't settle! We prosper and get paid better doing things we like. We excel in a path that we love and get paid better for it. Get ready to unleash your superpower and make the most of every moment!

6
Your Retirement Will Happen

Planning for retirement might not be the most exciting topic for young people, but it's an essential aspect of building a secure future. By setting goals, calculating your retirement expenses, harnessing the power of compound interest, and adopting smart saving strategies, you can take control of your financial future. Remember, the earlier you start, the more time you have to accumulate the money needed to retire comfortably. A nice age to retire is 60. Also studies indicate that people who retire early live longer and are more healthy too. So, start thinking about your retirement now and enjoy a worry-free and fulfilling future ahead!

However, when we stop earning money we need a way to pay those bills like electricity and food. Retirement is the phase of life when you stop working and rely on the savings and investments you've built over the years to cover your living expenses. It's like a long vacation but without the need to work!

Lessons from Regret: Elderly Perspectives on Retirement Funds

We can learn from the experiences of others that retired ahead of us. As you plan for your financial future, it's essential to understand the irreparable regrets that some elderly individuals have about their retirement funds. By learning from their mistakes, you can make smarter decisions and avoid potential pitfalls. In this section, we'll explore some common regrets expressed by the elderly regarding their retirement funds.

Insufficient Savings:
Many elderly individuals express regret about not saving enough for retirement. They often wish they had started saving earlier and contributed more consistently. So, remember, even small amounts saved regularly can add up over time. Start setting aside a portion of your income as early as possible, as this will help ensure a more secure retirement.

Ignoring Retirement Planning:

Some regret not actively engaging in retirement planning. It's crucial to create a retirement plan that includes setting goals, estimating expenses, and understanding the steps needed to achieve financial security. By neglecting this process, individuals may find themselves unprepared when retirement arrives. Take charge of your financial future by learning about retirement planning and seeking guidance if needed.

Reliance on Social Security:

While Social Security provides valuable support, relying solely on it can lead to regret later in life. Many elderly individuals express disappointment that their Social Security benefits alone weren't sufficient to cover their expenses comfortably. Understand that Social Security is designed to supplement your retirement savings, not replace it entirely. By building your own savings, you can enjoy a more financially stable retirement.

Risky Investments:

Regret is often expressed by those who took unnecessary risks with their retirement funds. Investing in speculative ventures without understanding the associated risks can lead to significant losses. It's crucial to educate yourself about different investment options, seek professional advice if needed, and diversify your investments to mitigate risk. It's okay to have some risky investments after you know how much is at stake. The most important part is risk allocation: only put money in risky places if you can lose that money. Will you still be on target for your retirement if the risky one utterly fails?

Lack of Contingency Planning:

The absence of contingency planning is another regret voiced by some elderly individuals. Sometimes, unexpected things can happen that mess up your retirement savings. It could be things like getting sick or the economy going downhill. To be prepared for these situations, it's a good idea to save up some money for emergencies. Also, think about getting insurance, like health insurance and long-term care insurance. That way, you'll have some backup when things get tough.

Summing Up:
Learning from the regrets of those who came before us can be a valuable lesson in preparing for our own financial future. By taking proactive steps to save consistently, engaging in retirement planning, avoiding overreliance on Social Security, making informed investment decisions, and planning for unexpected circumstances, you can increase your chances of a fulfilling and financially secure retirement. The best day to start was yesterday. Today is also a good time to start. The fact is it's never too early to start planning for your future, so seize the opportunity and set yourself up for retirement without regrets.

Real People have stories

It's easy enough to find a real person that failed to plan or to act on a plan. The following is a story based on a real person's life experience.

Once upon a time, there was a woman named Alicia. Alicia was a hardworking individual who dedicated most of her life to her job, always striving to provide for her family. She loved her work and enjoyed the present without thinking too much about the future.

As Alicia approached her retirement age, she started to realize that she hadn't saved enough for her golden years. You could say she had more years than gold. She didn't have a substantial retirement fund or a solid plan in place. It dawned on her that the dreams she had for her retirement might not become a reality.

Alicia's regret stemmed from the fact that she didn't prioritize saving for retirement when she was younger. It wasn't something in her awareness. She was caught up in the day-to-day expenses and didn't think about the long-term implications. While she enjoyed the present, she didn't realize the importance of balancing it with planning for the future.

She realized that she could have started saving even small amounts of money earlier on, which would have given her more time for her savings to grow. Alicia wished she had taken the time to learn about retirement planning and perhaps sought guidance from professionals who could have helped her make informed decisions.

Alicia's story teaches us an essential lesson: retirement happens and are we ready for it? As teenagers and young adults, we have the advantage of time on our side. By taking small steps now, such as saving a portion of our income regularly, we can set ourselves up for a more financially secure future.

Alicia's regret also highlights the significance of balancing our present desires with our future needs. While it's important to enjoy life and spend money on things that bring us joy, we shouldn't overlook the importance of saving and planning for the long term.

It's up to you to build your foundation for a bright and worry-free retirement.

Saving Strategies:
Saving for retirement doesn't mean you have to sacrifice all your fun and enjoyment now. It's about finding a balance between spending and saving. Here are a few strategies you can adopt:

1. Start small: Even saving a small percentage of your income each month can make a significant difference over time. Consider opening a retirement account, such as an Individual Retirement Account (IRA) or a 401(k) if available. In Canada, there is a Tax Free Saving Plan (TFSA) where any interest you earn on your investment is tax free, however there are certain guidelines that must be adhered too.

2. Automate your savings: Set up automatic transfers from your paycheck or checking account to your retirement savings account. This way, you won't even miss the money you're putting aside.

3. Minimize debt: High-interest debt can eat away at your savings. Make it a priority to pay off any outstanding debts, such as credit card balances or student loans, as early as possible.

4. Learn about investing: Educate yourself about different investment options, such as stocks. Consider seeking guidance from a financial advisor to make informed investment decisions.

The Power of Compound Interest:
One of the greatest advantages of starting to save for retirement early is the magic of compound interest. We've looked at this in the first chapter. Compound interest allows your money to grow exponentially over time. By investing your savings wisely, you can earn interest on your initial investment and the interest it generates. The longer your money stays invested, the more it will grow, so it pays to start saving as soon as possible.

Inflation Ate Your Lunch

The Rising Tide: Understanding Inflation and the Diminishing Power of Money

Have you ever wondered why the prices of things keep going up over time? Well, it's because of an old and pervasive phenomenon called inflation. Inflation affects the value of money and how much you can buy with it. Here we'll dive into the impact of inflation, explain how it affects your purchasing power, and give you a tangible example to help you grasp its impact.

What is Inflation?
Inflation is the gradual increase in the prices of goods and services over time. It means that the same amount of money will buy you less in the future than it does today. While a little bit of inflation is considered normal and even necessary for a healthy economy, too much inflation can erode the value of your hard-earned money.

Purchasing Power:
Purchasing power is the ability of your money to buy goods and services. When inflation occurs, the purchasing power of money diminishes because you need more money to buy the same things. Think of it as a tide slowly rising, making things more expensive as time goes on.

A Tangible Example:
To understand how inflation affects the value of money, let's take a look at a common item: a movie ticket. Around 50 years ago, you could enjoy a movie in a theater for just 69 cents. Fast forward to today, and the average cost of a movie ticket has risen significantly. What once cost under a dollar now often requires much more money from your pocket. That's the gradual effect of inflation in action.

Causes of Inflation:
Inflation can be caused by various factors. One primary factor is the increase in the cost of production, such as wages, raw materials, and energy. When businesses face higher costs, they often pass them on to consumers by raising prices. So you pay more for the same thing you bought last year. Additionally, changes in government policies, such as monetary policies and fiscal decisions, can also influence inflation rates. The easy one to notice is the interest rate banks give for your savings and the rate they charge on mortgages and credit cards. When that rate rises, inflation increases too.

Coping with Inflation:
While you can't stop inflation from happening, there are ways to cope with its effects. We've looked at these things before, but I'm saying it in a slightly different way and combining a few concepts.

Saving and Investing:
Saving money is essential, but it's also important to invest your savings wisely. By putting your money into investments that can outpace inflation, such as stocks, or real estate you can protect the value of your savings and even grow it over time. In another view, real estate is an asset. It takes money to buy that asset. Money is losing power but the asset remains strong. Shares in a company also hold

value while cash in a drawer loses its value. You can't slow down the sinking value of cash. We need to put cash into something that holds value and perhaps generates an income for us.

Fancy Cars Aren't Assets:
Cars diminish in value quickly. They don't hold value at all. A house keeps its value better. Look around at things that lose value or hold their value. These are easy things to explore by comparing an old price and a new price. For example, if you had silver or gold, what was the price of that 20 years ago and now? Compare that with movie tickets or something else that cost money.

Financial Education:
Understanding the basics of personal finance and investing can help you make informed decisions. Explore books, online resources, or even consider taking a personal finance course to gain knowledge about managing your money effectively. You can search the internet for inflation. It's very interesting to see the price of a house in 1950 versus now. You can ask a grandparent how much they paid for a house. You might wonder, how did they get it so cheap? Well, you can then ask how much people got paid for an average job (like bus driver). Then you see the shrinking "value" of money versus the rising value of assets.

Budgeting and Smart Spending:
By creating a budget and tracking your expenses, you can prioritize your spending and avoid unnecessary purchases. Being a smart shopper and seeking out the best deals can also help stretch your money further. This extra money needs to be invested, not sitting in cash.

Diversify Income Streams:
Consider exploring ways to earn additional income, such as part-time jobs, freelance work, or starting a small business. Having multiple sources of income can provide a cushion against the impact of inflation. However, don't run yourself into the ground trying to earn more and more money.

Learn to Live Simply:
If the expenses are lower (money going out), you don't need to make as much now, or in the future.

Reflections:
Understanding inflation and its impact on the value of money is crucial for your financial well-being. As prices rise over time, your purchasing power will diminish. However, by saving, investing, staying financially informed, budgeting, and diversifying your income streams, you can navigate the effects of inflation and ensure a stronger financial future. Being informed and proactive with your money will empower you to stay ahead of the rising tide of inflation! Money (cash) will lose value with inflation.

It's been a very long time since money increased in purchasing power. That's called deflation. The last time it happened the government created stimulus packages. That means you can expect inflation because the government will fight against deflation.

Investments that outperform inflation

There are generally two areas that outperform the stock market during inflationary times. This opinion is based on looking at 100 years of data.

1. Trending stocks and industries. Naturally "what" is trending depends on the current influences and disruptive technologies. They are easy to find with a little effort.
2. Commodities. These are typically the things that cost more during inflation: e.g. Oil, metals. I'm not recommending a new investor seek trading in the commodities "futures" markets. It's much simpler to buy shares in companies that produce or distribute commodities.

It's important to note that the price of stock shares includes the expectation of future profits and their current assets on the books. When inflation takes a turn up or down, the share prices turn sharply too, and one must remember to be agile in the ups and downs of the market.

One sentence pretty much sums it up, Money that "sleeps" shrinks. We need to hold assets that increase in value.

The Most Common Plan

A common retirement plan is to buy a house and pay off the mortgage over time. This idea has been used for 100 years by many people. Imagine owning a house that you can call your own, free from the burden of monthly rent payments. It sounds great, right? Well, it does have its pros and cons to consider.

By paying off your mortgage before retirement, you eliminate the need to make regular housing payments, which can be a significant expense for many people. This can free up your retirement income for other expenses and allow you to have more financial stability. Plus, owning a home can give you a sense of security and a place to call your own.

Even when you own it 100%, there are still ongoing costs to consider. In short, what pays for the food and electricity when the house is paid? There are still expenses for the house "upkeep," broken dishwashers, and annual property tax.

The second most common plan is to buy more than one house. Live in one and rent out the other. That accomplishes two things.

One, it provides you with a place to live while generating rental income from the other property. This additional income can help offset your living expenses and contribute towards your retirement savings. Renting out a property can be a stable source of passive income, especially if you carefully select a desirable location and manage the property effectively. There is a risk with tenants that may cause damage to your property. Picking a good tenant is a skill.

Two, owning multiple properties can also serve as a long-term investment. Real estate has the potential to appreciate over time, meaning the value of your properties may increase. As you approach retirement, you can choose to sell one or more properties to supplement your retirement funds or continue renting them out for ongoing income. Diversifying your assets by investing in real estate can provide financial stability and potential growth, adding a layer of security to your retirement strategy.

However, it's important to consider the responsibilities and risks associated with owning rental properties. Being a landlord requires active management, including finding reliable tenants after one leaves, handling maintenance and repairs, and staying updated on local rental laws. Additionally, the real estate market can be unpredictable, therefore thorough research and analysis are crucial before purchasing additional properties. It's advisable to consult with professionals, such as real estate agents and financial advisors, to ensure this strategy aligns with your financial goals and risk tolerance.

The only recent change in the quality of this plan is the declining birth rate. With the declining birth rate in many countries, it's vital to pay attention to the type of second house you consider for rental income during retirement. As the population ages and the number of potential tenants decreases, it becomes increasingly important to choose a property that aligns with the changing needs of the population. For instance, opting for a smaller, more accessible home or a property located in areas with high demand from retirees could be a wise choice. Additionally, considering the preferences and lifestyle trends of the aging population, such as proximity to healthcare facilities, recreational activities, and amenities tailored to their needs, can help ensure a steady rental income and maximize the value of your investment. By adapting to the evolving demographic landscape, you can make informed decisions about the second house you buy, ensuring its attractiveness and long-term rental potential in a changing market.

Chapter Summary

Your investing and savings need to last longer than you do during retirement. Running out of money and being too old to earn more is devastating. Unfortunately, this happens to thousands of Americans every year. Let's not be one of those people.

7
Sustained Motivation

Do you aspire to achieve your dreams? I believe 85% of success lies in having a clear vision of what you want. Sounds simple, right? Well, it is! And I'm here to help you make the most of your goals and motivation.

Think about it this way: investing just a few minutes into the goals and motivation department will save you loads of time and get you to your destination faster. The masters of success always keep themselves sharp by staying focused on what they want. Also, it's important to understand that being sharp isn't being obsessed.

You see, nearly all successful people set goals and stay motivated. Those who neglect this crucial step miss out on opportunities to be adaptable and creative. Sometimes, staying focused on the goal, rather than the process, can actually shorten the path to success.

Life is full of opportunities and challenges, and having a flexible approach to reaching your goals while staying true to your values can save you a lot of time. For instance, think about why you're doing something. Are you in business because it's what you've always done, or is it to have more time with your family? How you frame your actions is more important than the actions themselves. Being aware of your purpose can prevent mistakes and open doors to amazing opportunities. Remember: Keep your mind on the goal, not just the process.

Successful people understand that the key to success lies in defining their motivation. Knowing 'why' you're pursuing something is far more important than knowing 'how' to get there. Most successful people can tell you all about the unexpected twists and turns they encountered on their journey. Their goals were clear, but the path was filled with surprises.

I want you to create goals that serve your best interests and those of the people in your life. This is your life, after all. Don't let good ideas simply remain ideas. Implement them! A good idea put into action has the potential to make a billion dollars, even if it starts small and takes years to grow. So, have a good idea, and don't be afraid to share it with others.

Remember the wise words of John Lennon: 'A dream you dream alone is only a dream. A dream you dream together is reality.' So, dream big, involve others, and turn your dreams into reality!

Visualizing Your Success

The saying "what you see is what you get" holds true when it comes to having a vision. Only by envisioning a desired outcome does it become a possibility.

A few years back, I had the opportunity to take a professional driving course, specifically for race car driving. During the course, I learned a valuable lesson: The wheels of a car often follow the direction in which the driver is **looking**. It surprised me how simple and accurate this concept was. It required a conscious effort to resist this instinctive behavior. However, it was much easier to embrace this truth and focus my gaze on where I wanted the car to go. I adopted a new habit they taught called "high vision," which involved looking farther ahead on the road (quite literally) rather than just a few feet past the car's hood. Interestingly, drivers who follow this advice from professionals tend to have fewer accidents. By looking further ahead and focusing on where you want to go, you enhance your driving skills and overall safety.

This lesson extends beyond driving. It applies to life in general. When we have a clear vision of our desired destination, we are more likely to reach it. By looking ahead and focusing on where we want to go, we naturally align our actions and decisions with our ultimate goals. Just as professional drivers keep their eyes on the road ahead, we too should keep our sights on the bigger picture. So, remember to visualize your success, set your gaze on your desired path, and make conscious efforts to move in that direction.

Who says you are Small?

Who are they to say you're small? Don't let the limited thinking of others hinder your path to success. There will always be "nay-sayers," but why should you pay them any mind? If the people around you aren't providing useful guidance and support, it's time to change your environment.

Imagine if Thomas Edison had listened to everyone else; he would have only invented a better candle. You see, at the age of 14, John Lennon, the legendary Beatles member, was told by his mother to discard his poetry because "You can't make money as a poet." Yet, John went on to become the highest-paid poet of all time. Just think about all the people who have been moved by his songs. His mother may have thought he was a dreamer, but he certainly wasn't the only one.

When someone tells you, "You can't do this," remember that they're simply guessing. In reality, they might be saying that they can't do it or that they can't envision it themselves. If John Lennon's mother had been a highly successful poet, then her statement might have held more weight. It would have been professional advice instead of uninformed criticism or mere speculation disguised as authority. If there's a knowledgeable critic genuinely striving to help me improve, they deserve my time and attention. But the opinions of others should be evaluated for their qualifications before accepting them.

"The more willing you are to let go of the stories of who you think you are, the more space there is for your true self to emerge." ~ Oprah Winfrey.

Embrace this opportunity for personal growth and self-discovery.

Everyone is self-made, but only successful people admit it.

I'm not diminishing the assistance of others that have helped me, especially when I was a baby or from teachers in school. This part is about the influence my attitudes have upon me. You really can learn from the simple acts in life. This book had many people giving great feedback to improve it.

Let me share with you a valuable lesson about success that I've learned while searching for a parking spot at a store. When I start thinking, "I never get a good parking spot near the entrance," chances are I'll end up driving to the back or middle of the parking lot. But if I change my belief, things start to shift. I drive closer to the entrance and actively search for a nearby spot.

You see, my belief directly influences my actions, shaping the choices I make. The outcomes I experience are limited to the possibilities I allow myself to see. It's impossible to find a fantastic parking spot near the front if I'm only focused on the back of the lot. That belief becomes my reality, and eventually, I find myself saying, "I never get a spot up front," all because of the choices I made. The other important part of this truth lies in the lack of effort—by not actively seeking, I missed out on creating an opportunity for myself, all because of my belief.

What you believe can have a significant impact on the choices you make and the opportunities you create. Keep an open mind, challenge your beliefs, and be proactive in seeking the outcomes you desire. Success often starts with the right mindset and the willingness to create your own opportunities.

Taking Action and Achieving Goals

The barrier between potential and actual accomplishments lies within doubts and fears. It is the single word "can" that differentiates "can do" and "doing", and wields the power to drive us ahead or stay stagnant. Many incredible accomplishments have been achieved by individuals who had fears and doubts. It's important to note that what may seem like a great feat to others can be something simple but significant to oneself; such as a dark-skinned slave in the 1800s USA becoming an independent business person. It was a remarkable achievement for their family.

Confidence in our abilities varies among individuals. The key is to move past hesitation and turn "can do" into reality ("done") by taking action.

Setbacks and failures are an inherent part of life. However, the real adventure lies in trying and the effort exerted along the way. Failing to achieve a specific goal doesn't equate to failure as long as an effort was made. Living life as an adventure, and embracing the journey, is what truly matters. The only true failure is not living life as an adventure. Playing it safe is merely storing life away. Is that really fulfilling?

The availability of tools and information isn't the main issue for most people. The problem often lies in their thinking patterns. Books like "As a Man Thinketh" by James Allen delve into this topic extensively.

The second most common problem is taking action based on the information we have. It requires making a decision. Taking risks entails a percentage of success, whereas inaction guarantees no success at all.

The third most prevalent problem is committing to seeing our goals through to completion. Persistence is a well-known principle of success. If people give up before even starting, it's likely because they approached their goals with a mere sense of "that's a good idea." However, a "good idea" lacks compelling value unless it becomes a tangible value that can be almost tasted.

Virtual food doesn't nourish a real stomach. To translate a goal into actionable steps, it must become more than just an abstract concept like "that's cool" or "I'd like that." Commitment is essential, and it stems from having a clear "why." During the journey of turning goals into reality, doubts and distractions will arise. Sustained action requires a strong underlying reason for doing the work. It's worth emphasizing: All wealth begins in the heart and mind, but it requires action to manifest in physical form.

In essence, the common ingredients for success are setting goals, making decisions, and following through. It seems simple, so why don't more people do it? In the United States, immigrants are four times more likely to achieve success compared to those born there. This indicates that it's not solely about opportunity but also about individuals' desires for success. It's their "why" that drives them. The desire can arise from awareness or life experiences. The will to succeed ultimately rests with the individual, while others may simply sigh and say, "It's too hard or requires too much work."

Is the Universe Friendly?

Is the universe on our side? Albert Einstein, renowned for his scientific brilliance, was also a deep thinker and philosopher. His genius extended far beyond science. Imagine someone capable of writing different math formulas simultaneously with both hands. That's the level of intellectual prowess we're talking about here. Now, imagine that same mind pondering the profound aspects of life. According to Einstein, the most important thing we need to know is whether the universe is fundamentally friendly or not.

If we believe the universe, or even certain parts of it, is unsafe, that belief will shape our actions and choices. As we've seen earlier, our beliefs have the power to limit our reality. We might end up living in fear, isolating ourselves within secure but confining walls.

If you're struggling to determine whether the universe is friendly, you can adopt Einstein's perspective. It took me a while to fully embrace this belief. In our society, many people have been conditioned to live in fear. However, other cultures at different times didn't hold that belief. They were able to enjoy life more fully simply because they felt safe. Some individuals might argue for the virtues of fear and safety, but I believe that the logical consequences of our actions are distinct from the unproductive and unhealthy emotion of fear.

We've all experienced events that seem negative at first. However, if those experiences teach us valuable lessons that enhance our lives, can they truly be considered negative? If we survive and learn from an experience, doesn't that make us more capable than before? If there are significant experiences from which we haven't gleaned significant lessons, perhaps those lessons will come back to us in a stronger form until we grasp them. Sometimes, major tragedies serve as lessons for others too. For instance, the United Nations Declaration of Human Rights was born out of great tragedy, with a few individuals transforming it into a higher standard for humanity's well-being. However, it's crucial to acknowledge that this standard isn't upheld everywhere. If it's not being upheld where you live, why remain there? There are opportunities available when we actively seek them, just like finding a parking spot up front by the door.

Where do your wounds lie? Only in memories. Remarkable individuals with disabilities are living extraordinary lives. We must examine our wounds to extract the lessons within them and free ourselves from the painful parts of our memories.

Remember, above the clouds, the sun always shines. Even in the darkest times, if we can be patient, the sun will shine again. It has been doing so for three billion years. We don't need to worry about changing its batteries; imagine the government programs required for that task! Life is good if we choose to see it that way. We shape our past, present, and future through the stories we tell—our beliefs, perceptions, and preselected choices.

Since you will inevitably form an opinion, and the facts remain the same, why not cultivate an opinion that serves you better? It's up to you to shape your perspective and create a narrative that empowers you.

Eliminating Fear

Fear can be likened to an aerosol spray, releasing a lingering scent that stays with us for a long time. Similarly, it doesn't take much to trigger our neurons and feel fear coursing through our bodies. This response is partly due to our programming and upbringing. However, our perception of fear can help reduce its impact. Let's take a moment to examine fear because it often obstructs rational thinking. For many people, fear puts an end to taking action. It's important to note that this is not about being reckless and acting unwisely despite fear. We're focusing on understanding the mechanics of fear.

During a survival event, specific centers in our brains become activated and take control. Survival can mean the continuation of our species, our family, or ourselves. It's helpful at times. If we see a falling baby we automatically react with our instincts to save it. This is where one part of our brain overrides everything else that's happening just then. It's a good feature.

That same brain feature can cause road rage; an example of how an otherwise calm and rational person can become highly emotional and compelled to attack a stranger. It's not a rational response, and unfortunately, it seems to take over and persist for a while. Understanding the mechanics of fear is important because it can feel overpowering and is generally unstoppable once triggered.

The power to control these irrational, primal reactions begins with perception. We'll keep our perceptions about falling babies but road rage is an example of altering perceptions and deflecting instantaneous reactions. If the driver in a road rage situation were to perceive things differently, the survival instincts would not be triggered. I agree that it feels like our lives are occasionally threatened by other reckless drivers who make mistakes or aren't attentive on the road. Distractions like cell phones and busy lives contribute to this.

So, how can we calm the survival instinct when there's a real threat to our safety? Well, there's only one way I know of, and that's through pre-acceptance of the outcome. I've observed that acceptance is one path to finding peace. Acceptance doesn't mean that we prefer a certain outcome; it means acknowledging that life will eventually come to an end, possibly through a random event. Accepting the worst possible outcome brings us peace and reduces fear. I accept the possibility that an inattentive driver may be on the road when I am, but I still choose to travel, knowing that possibility exists. As a pre-plan, it's my "program" to move out of the way. I have pre-decided this and have visualized it so that part of my brain will follow the program. Using logic I know retaliating isn't the best choice and they won't truly learn anything from it either. The logical pre-plan is to move away from it. This needs to be converted into automated behavior using visualization and being accepting of the way the world is.

Pre-acceptance of certain things leads to peace. I also apply the principle of acceptance when there's no choice in a matter. Accepting something that lacks options isn't about giving up or resigning; it's a wise decision given the absence of choices. I redirect my energy towards things I do have a choice about.

In some cases, a new fear may arise without the opportunity for pre-acceptance. However, I always have time afterward to process the fearful aspects. Fear is subjective, and someone else might not share the same perspective. It's not about being right or wrong in terms of the circumstances; what matters is quelling the erratic and illogical reaction to those circumstances. Of course, it's natural to feel angry or sad at times—such is life. The problem lies in the survival-driven perceptions that hinder cognitive processing. Brain 1.0, with its old designs, activates the survival centers instead of the cognitive ones. This, we can't change.

To process emotions effectively, we need emotional intelligence. By processing old fears over time and gaining wisdom, we can cope better in the present moment. Our perceptions can evolve to "This isn't a threat."

If we want brain 2.0 to operate, we must preconceive most situations as acceptable. Pre-acceptance of life's challenges helps maintain a sense of calm; preventing the triggering of survival "fight or flight".

Another way to dissipate every day fearful feelings is through gratitude. Gratitude is a higher state of being than mere acceptance. When fear dissipates, abundance can manifest. Removing fear allows life to flow into us without restraint. We can even start the process of abundance the other way around—by cultivating gratitude first. It can be as simple as finding one thing to compliment someone about, initiating an amazing habit.

A quick fix is to change the type of music and movies going into our minds. Music is a mood reinforcement tool.

The Power of Having a Strong Purpose

Motivation is a powerful tool for action. It's essential to channel it towards personal goals that resonate with our sense of purpose. By doing this, our actions become meaningful and fulfilling, rather than solely for the benefit of others. Discovering our true purpose in life takes time and can seem like a complex process. I spent decades pondering this question, as it is open-ended and subjective. Determining what constitutes a meaningful purpose can be challenging, especially when we encounter conflicting opinions from various sources. It's important to be selective about whose perspectives we listen to.

In a world characterized by limitless opportunities, brimming with more information than we can possibly retain, endless places to explore and people to meet, setting priorities becomes paramount. Without a well-defined set of guiding principles, we risk being swept away by the overwhelming array of choices and distractions, seeking substitutes while our true purpose remains unfulfilled. Only by anchoring ourselves with our core values can we begin to navigate this vast ocean with clarity and intention.

As the saying goes, "If you don't stand for something, you'll fall for anything." When faced with difficulties, we can weigh them against our life's purpose. Some things may not be worth pursuing because they don't align with what truly matters to us, while others are worth fighting for. These choices are ours to make. It could be as simple as prioritizing eating carrots over strawberry cheesecake when hunger strikes.

Ultimately, it is you who defines your life. Whatever beliefs or religious practices you follow, they are based on your personal choices and reasons. Maximize your life's potential, it requires reevaluating past decisions and determining whether they still hold. In the world of investments, for instance, what may have been a great idea once might not be as promising anymore due to changing circumstances. We live in a universe of constant change, and adaptability is one of the most valuable skills we can possess. While there are certain universal rules governing our existence (like gravity and magnetism), having a purpose and adapting to changes are key aspects of navigating life successfully. Your purpose is entirely your own to choose.

Recognizing that it is impossible to "do it all," we must accept that we will live in only a few locations, engage in a limited range of activities, and make selective choices. Drifting through life without intentional decision-making is acceptable, but you may find greater fulfillment by directing your life's trajectory while embracing adaptability.

Life can be likened to a sport—either you're on the field actively participating or sitting on the sidelines as a commentator. The "good idea" people are like commentators, observing and analyzing from a distance. Where do you want to be?

It is common for many individuals to feel uneasy about taking charge of their lives. The world needs more leaders, and leading your own life means that someone else isn't doing it for you. You are the captain of your own ship, and acknowledging this fact empowers you to move forward.

If we possess cognitive abilities and various senses but fail to utilize them, we are squandering valuable opportunities. It's akin to being a walking and talking houseplant, gifted with breath, time, mobility, and energy. Energy is abundant because we have enough nourishment to fuel our bodies; it all comes down to the choices we make. Our choices are often limited due to our habits, but embracing new choices can feel uncomfortable simply because they are unfamiliar. Be bold and embrace the opportunity to do something new.

Chapter Summary

Big fish grow in big waters. To be a "big fish" you need room to grow. That translates to expanding your mind, reducing self-criticism, self-doubt, and limiting habits.

8
Achieving the Goal

If you're already deeply motivated, then you can skip this chapter.

Getting Off Track

Ever wondered why distractions can throw us off course? It's like working on someone else's goal instead of our own. But is that really okay? Let's break it down. The word "distraction" can give us a clue. "Dis" means "not," as in "dis-connected" means not connected. And "traction" is what propels us forward. So, when we're dis-tracted, we're not moving forward.

The next time you find yourself distracted, remember that it can hinder your progress. It's alright if you let it, but think about this: Did you give it proper attention, or did you just get pulled in by your habits? If it's the latter, it's time to ask yourself: When should distractions be reassessed to see if they deserve my time and attention?

The decisions we make shape our lives. Without making decisions, we might end up drifting aimlessly without a clear direction. If we don't take control of our own lives, someone else will, or worse, we'll be stuck in a waking coma. So, when a distraction comes along, go back to your goals and get back on track. Of course, goals need to be balanced with our values. For example, is spending time with family a distraction or a core value? Sometimes, establishing boundaries with their consent is the key to achieving your goals. Remember, this isn't about being selfish or giving up everything—it's about sharing a vision that aligns with your dreams.

Creating a Positive Mindset

Our surroundings, distractions, and mindset shape who we become.

One important habit I've developed is giving attention to the language I use. In an earlier chapter, we looked at our internal dialog. Here I want to briefly show the relationship to motivation and feelings. When we anticipate a positive emotional response, taking action becomes effortless. Conversely, if we don't feel inclined to do something, we tend to avoid it.

Our deliberate vocalization, the words we choose, will drive our feelings too. And thus the actions we might take that shape our future.

Feelings that repeat become moods. Moods become a personality. Personality circles back into who we identify as. My grandmother would say about someone "They are a sour person." She just named the personality she encountered.

Since feelings affect us, I would challenge myself to reevaluate the words I used sometimes. I'm the source of my words. I'm affected by them too. Specifically, I'd look at the worn-out words I used that have lost their motivational influence on me. This attention to what I say would help me be engaged with my goals. Just watching my words when I spoke and listened. For instance, the word "positive" no longer carried the same weight it once did for me. To keep me focused, I occasionally explored alternative expressions. I was trying to rewire my feelings related to words and keep them lively. I didn't do this challenge after I rewired my feelings to be always positive. I grew up in a negative home with negative words. I'm around me all the time, so I wanted a certain calm happy vibe for me. Now, people pick up my vibe (the one I honed for me) when we meet.

My feelings will motivate me. The words are reminders tied to feelings. The constant feeling ("pervasive mood") I have includes: Am I doing something useful or not? And having fun is useful too. It's not about being productive all the time. Yet having some fun is productive in the big picture. We need that too. The feeling is put more clearly: Am I on purpose with my life?

Achieving Success: Overcoming Challenges

It's commonly believed that the smartest individuals should be the wealthiest. After all, their intelligence should enable them to anticipate and capitalize on upcoming trends. However, I noticed a curious phenomenon while coaching people for stock market success. Contrary to expectations, the smartest individuals often underperformed compared to those with average intelligence. Interestingly, women frequently outperformed men, giving me an insight into success.

So, what is it that smart people need to know to attain the success they deserve? And what did a few women do differently to achieve substantial success?

The challenge that smart individuals face is their heightened awareness of risks. This awareness often leads them to avoid taking risks altogether, which may seem like a smart decision from their perspective. However, the missing ingredient for their success lies in their ability to perceive a way around the risks and take action. The fear of failure (and looking stupid) becomes a significant barrier to their success.

Commonly the fear of appearing foolish or making a mistake holds smart individuals back. The potential embarrassment that comes with failure is particularly distressing for them, as their identity is strongly tied to their intelligence. The greatest risk lies in fear of looking foolish, which ultimately leads to the failure of inaction.

Their hesitation to start a project due to this fear is what ultimately leads to failure—failure to produce anything or utilize their unique gift of intelligence. Unfortunately, this aspect is often overlooked when weighing the decision of whether to pursue a goal or not. I recommend a good book "Curse of the High IQ" by Aaron Clarey.

On the other hand, women at my stock trading classes experienced greater success simply by following instructions. They didn't feel the need to improve the system since "the wheel is already round." On average, they were more inclined to adhere to established systems compared to men. It appears that men often sought to figure things out on their own and add their changes. It's not that men possessed more knowledge than the coaches or women; it was a matter of cultural conditioning. Generally, men are taught to be self-reliant, whereas women are encouraged to seek help from trusted sources. Women rely on information networks built through discussions or from grocery store magazines for example. This process was for their best interest, while men typically turn to technical references and figure things out independently. These cultures were normal before the 2000s.

This cultural programming is evident in situations where men hesitate to ask for directions when they are lost. They follow their social conditioning of self-dependence. Many social messages still reinforce this notion of men being the sole breadwinners and standing strong for the entire team. Although society has evolved, these messages from the 1980s and earlier still linger in the minds of individuals over forty. It becomes evident when a trigger such as a TV jingle or a line from an old movie script sparks an immediate response. For instance, try completing this sentence: "Go ahead punk, make my _____." Most older adult males automatically fill in the blank with "day" in their heads. It's challenging not to say it. Imagine saying the alternative: "Go ahead punk, make my sandwich." It feels different, doesn't it?

Here are some steps you can take right now:
- Understand that your influence only extends to your fingertips. The rest is up to the Universe.
- Practice self-forgiveness for your mistakes. Embrace the idea that your life can be seen as "The Adventures of My Life." Just like Bilbo Baggins, everyone makes mistakes, and that's how we learn. Seek additional resources on forgiveness to deepen your understanding.
- Cultivate a non-judgmental mindset towards others. By doing so, you create space to "be" and explore different possibilities in life.
- Expect and accept mistakes and move on with the lessons learned.

Remember, success is not solely determined by intelligence but also by our ability to navigate challenges, be resilient, overcome fears, and embrace continuous growth.

The Power of Fair Exchange

If there is one crucial aspect to understand for success, it would be the concept of "fair exchange." In our economy-driven world, almost everything is valued in comparison to other things. This fundamental truth has been evident since ancient times through the existence of merchants and commerce.

While the principles of commerce are well-established, they are not always well-explained. Some individuals have had better access to these principles, as seen when wealthy families pass down their wealth and the knowledge of managing and growing it. Unfortunately, not everyone has embraced these multi-generational wealth-building principles or has forgotten them, resulting in the loss of family wealth.

Similar to the undeniable force of gravity, arguing against well-established success principles is futile and wasteful. It is easier to work in harmony with these principles and utilize them to our advantage. Ignorance of these principles only hinders progress.

At the core of success in commerce lies the principle of fair exchange. An ancient mercantile saying goes, "Fair is anything that two people agree upon." It means that an exchange is considered fair when both parties involved agree on the terms at that specific moment. This principle forms the foundation of contract law, where the "meeting of the minds" is essential. It ensures that both parties understand and agree on the nature of the exchange. If any misunderstandings arise, there are mechanisms in place to address and resolve them.

Contract law, like commerce, permeates various aspects of our lives. A contract can be as simple as an agreement to "take out the garbage" in exchange for preparing dinner, or a promise to take someone to Disneyland if they achieve an "A" in biology. In essence, the more people we provide a service to, the greater our chances of success. By delivering exceptional value to a vast number of people, we receive substantial value in return. This is the essence of fairness. "Much is given, much is received."

For the purpose of this discussion, let's set aside the existence of those who use deceit to acquire what they don't deserve. Their actions do not align with the principles of fair dealings.

You may have noticed that this information is not being presented as a flashy revelation that you must urgently acquire ("operators are standing by... call now"). It doesn't need to be flashy because it is rooted in truth and effectiveness. Flashy tactics aim to alter perceived value rather than discuss actual value.

Psychological and marketing tools have been employed in sales to extract more money from our pockets, creating the illusion of a fair exchange. However, such perceived value manipulation has existed for centuries, resulting in unfair deals. Ever heard the expression "Caveat emptor" (buyer beware)? It is not a new concept. The problem with relying on perceived value is that it ultimately undermines moral integrity and tarnishes reputations. Many people prioritize their bank accounts and appearances of wealth over the value of their soul/heart connection and true substance.

Allow me to illustrate the importance of providing value with an example. While on a trip, I encountered a homeless man living in a park in Belize City. He asked for money, but I offered him a banana instead. I refrained from giving money as I knew that it would likely be used for drugs, which perpetuates an unhealthy cycle. Offering a banana, which is unlikely to be sold, was my alternative. On this occasion, he declined the banana but expressed a desire to converse. We spent about an hour sitting under the afternoon sun, during which he shared his story; how he ended up in his current situation, and his aspirations. He expressed a desire to accumulate wealth and lead a comfortable life in old age. He is currently 40 years old.

The questions I posed to him might seem simple and obvious to you. "How will you achieve your goals if you continue doing what you're doing? What value do you offer to others? If you give nothing, why should anyone give anything to you? And if you receive some help, what will you do with it?"

Naturally, the money given to him would dissipate, leading to his continued dependence on assistance. He lacked the habit of sustaining or growing wealth. It's important to recognize that our income and outcomes are determined by our habits and the value we provide through our actions.

We discussed his past experience of washing windshields in Los Angeles, where he received tips from people. He offered a service and, in return, sometimes received something of value.

We met a few more times in the park, enjoying our conversations. We delved into the simplicity and value of his windshield-washing service. I firmly believe that he possesses all the necessary tools to succeed if he takes action and provides value. Now, the choice is his to make. In the end, I remain uncertain about the path he will choose in life. I've included an appendix on the difference between Compassion and Empathy. We will have feelings about homeless people. The appendix looks at those similar words.

We do not require anything more than this understanding. What are we waiting for? If you're waiting for something flashy to ignite your drive, it's up to you to provide that spark. Only you can offer a compelling enough reason to initiate and sustain your journey. This concept is covered in other chapters. And I want you to become the best version of yourself because we occupy the same planet. That's my selfish motive revealed. What you do in your part of the world may affect me.

Get Paid

Part of the training to build a wealthy retirement involves being compensated for the value we provide. While it may sound simple, many people deny themselves the opportunity to receive payment, often responding with "No, that's okay," and rejecting compensation. However, this creates an imbalance. When you provide a benefit, it is both mentally and financially healthy to be rewarded in some form. Failing to establish a reciprocal relationship perpetuates the imbalance, which can eventually lead to hidden pains or unfulfilled expectations. It's crucial to acknowledge that this imbalance exists, even if it's not immediately noticeable.

The universe, with it's approximate 100 billion galaxies, exhibits impeccable bookkeeping and profoundly intelligence. An example of universal intelligence is the flawless operation of all the electrons on the planet. The furniture maintains its integrity without my effort—it simply works. Physical matter adheres to its design. Electrons don't require vacations or therapy for stress relief, nor do they need school to learn how to function. They naturally follow the design of things.

Stress arises when there is resistance to this design. As complex beings with choices, we need to learn how to work with the universe; understanding its principles.

The universe is in a state of expansion, and two fundamental rules within it are growth and change. Resisting change equates to resisting growth, and that creates pain. The section on Fair Exchange in this book will provide guidance on these matters. However, I recommend reading all the chapters in sequence, as this book is structured to help you when read from front to back.

Accepting payment supports being in balance.

The Power of Time, Intelligence, and Mastery

Time is an unstoppable force, constantly propelling us forward. This simple truth has a profound impact on our lives. Consider the phrase "keeping up with the times."

If our knowledge doesn't expand along with the passage of time, our expertise will gradually diminish in comparison. On the other hand, if we continue to learn and grow, our expertise will improve and evolve over time.

When it comes to financial matters, most individuals acquire the basics and then cease their education. They make slight advancements in their careers, but they don't actively engage in reading or continuous learning once formal schooling is complete. However, you stand above the average because you're currently reading and seeking knowledge, and I encourage you to keep doing so.

Maintaining a functional level of knowledge is important, but it falls short of achieving mastery in a particular field. There's more to wealth than simply understanding credit cards.

I propose that most people possess only a basic understanding of banking, investments, income, and business. It's no surprise, then, that their income and wealth remain within the "basics." As James Allen emphasized in his book "As a Man Thinketh," an ancient principle holds true: You can only grow corn from corn seed. Basic knowledge creates basic outcomes.

Creating immense value, such as generating millions of dollars, requires a mindset focused on creating tremendous value for others. It stems from a mind that is dedicated to envisioning and implementing groundbreaking ideas that transform the lives of many. By expanding our thinking and continuously honing our skills, we can unlock the potential to create extraordinary value for ourselves and those around us.

Chapter Summary

Distractions can hinder our progress and steer us away from our goals. It's important to reassess distractions and determine if they deserve our time and attention. Making decisions and taking control of our own lives is crucial to avoid drifting aimlessly. Balancing goals with values and setting boundaries allows us to achieve our dreams while maintaining important relationships.

Our mindset and the words we use impact our feelings and actions.

Continuously learning and growing is essential to maintain expertise and achieve mastery in a particular field. Embracing these principles, providing value, and accepting fair compensation contribute to a balanced and successful life journey.

Appendix - Compassion or Empathy

Compassion and empathy are two related but different ways of understanding and connecting with the emotions of others. Let's explore the distinctions between them using examples:

Compassion:
- Compassion means recognizing when someone is suffering or in distress and genuinely wanting to help them feel better.
- For instance, imagine you see a homeless person on the street. If you feel compassion, you would not only understand that they are going through a tough time, but you would also feel a strong desire to do something to help, like buying them a warm meal.

Empathy:
- Empathy is about understanding and sharing the emotions of others. It means putting yourself in someone else's shoes and feeling what they are feeling.
- For example, let's say your friend is going through a difficult breakup. If you have empathy, you would be able to imagine how they are feeling and share in their sadness and pain because you can relate to their experience.

To summarize, compassion involves recognizing and addressing someone's suffering, while empathy focuses on understanding and sharing the emotions of others. Compassion often leads to taking action to help, while empathy is primarily about connecting with others emotionally. Both compassion and empathy are valuable qualities that help build positive relationships and support those in need.

9
Accelerating Your Path to Financial Freedom

Velocity is the speed at which things move, and in the realm of wealth, it plays a crucial role. In this chapter, we'll explore how you can take control of the velocity of your wealth, propelling you toward your financial goals at a faster pace.

At a minimum, the rate that your savings grow must beat inflation: the rising cost of food for example.

The Incredible Power of Compounding

Back in high school, I was introduced to the concept of compounding numbers. At the time, it didn't capture my attention because I failed to see its relevance to my life. However, years later, during a sales presentation on life insurance and mutual funds, I discovered the extraordinary power of compounding. It left such a profound impact on me that I considered becoming a sales representative solely to spread the word about the incredible potential of compounding with mutual funds. Fortunately, my focus on educating people about this principle rather than making sales made me an ineffective rep, leading me to leave the company. Nevertheless, the lessons I learned still resonate within me, and I'm determined to share this message on the power of compounding.

About a year later, I had the fortune of meeting a young and prosperous mortgage broker. I was Intrigued by his success and inquired about his strategies. He revealed that he had several doctors as clients, all seeking investments that yielded a remarkable 40% or more in returns. Such a high benchmark for return on investment seemed unimaginable at the time. As the sole provider for my young family, with limited disposable income, I didn't delve deeper into the topic.

Now, let's consider the combination of these two concepts: compounding and a 40% rate of return. The impact can be astounding for those who witness it firsthand. Numbers don't deceive; they are guided by pure mathematics. If you have money available for investment, this should ignite a spark within you to take action now.

For instance, a 7% return over 20 years would multiply your initial investment by 3.8 times. Starting with $1,000,000, it would grow to $3,869,684.46 without any additional effort. To simplify calculations, let's assume the interest is paid only once per year. If we raise the rate of return by just 1%, that same investment becomes 4.6 times larger. In the previous example, this would mean an **additional** $791,272.68. No extra work is required. You can validate these figures by using a "Compound Interest Calculator" available through a quick web search.

Now, brace yourself for this revelation: what if we achieved a 40% return per year? In traditional thinking, 40% is merely five times greater than 8%. Therefore, the result should be roughly five times the 4.6 we obtained from the 8% investment, right? Well, prepare to be amazed. A 40% return would transform $1,000,000 into a staggering sum of nearly a billion dollars: $836,682,554.25.

This is how Warren Buffet became a billionaire: a high rate of return compounded over decades.

This example illustrates that transitioning from being a millionaire to a billionaire is simply a matter of securing a favorable rate of return on your investments. I've personally encountered individuals who have achieved remarkable returns. However, it's important to note that such high returns are not readily available through typical web searches or accessible to the average person. Certain restrictions, such as becoming an accredited investor per SEC regulations, exist. Additionally, acquiring the skill to discern good investments from bad ones is necessary. Do you know the risks you are taking with an IPO?

Investing is no longer just a side gig for the average person; it has become an essential part of financial growth. The investor's role now entails learning about investment opportunities and discovering high-quality investments that offer superior returns beyond the commonly available options. That also means weeding out the good-looking but weak investments. Not easy, but it's a skill that can be learned and has been learned by many.

Moreover, there is much more to understand about banking. For example, as the value of your account increases, traditional banks may not be the safest place to keep your money. I have compelling stories to share with you from a fifth-generation banker, but unfortunately, I cannot repeat them in written format. However, I will give you the insights gained.

In the journey toward financial freedom, understanding the power of compounding and exploring alternative investment opportunities is paramount. By embracing these principles and expanding your knowledge, you can unleash the potential to accelerate your wealth velocity and create a brighter financial future.

The Bridge Between Income and Wealth

G. J. Santoni, a senior economist at the Federal Reserve Bank of St. Louis, wrote an article back in March 1987 that discussed an important concept: the difference between wealth and income. Let's dive into the main points of that article and explore the bridge that connects these two aspects. You'll see where you fit in.

Wealth refers to the sum of all your assets minus your liabilities ("debts"). It's a straightforward way to measure your net worth, which is something you might have heard of before.

Net Worth = Assets - Debts.

Now, when Santoni referred to income in his article, he specifically meant expected income, not things like bonuses or surprises. It's the money you anticipate earning.

But here's the part that I find fascinating: Santoni quotes Irving Fisher, an influential economist, who said that the bridge between wealth and income is the interest rate. This quote came from Fisher's book written in 1954, where he delves into the theory of interest.

In Fisher's book, he presents a unique perspective on capital and income. He considers everything from human labor to land and other forms of capital as income-producing assets. Fisher was one of the first to openly publish this idea that man's labor should be viewed on par with other assets. While there may have been earlier works exploring this notion, Fisher's boldness in grouping human labor with other assets is notable. Though it's worth mentioning that modern perspectives are often less inclined to lump human beings together with traditional assets.

Now, if you find yourself not yet a billionaire or millionaire, and sometimes struggle to make ends meet, this next part might be valuable to you. Let's put aside any concerns about being treated as an "asset" for a moment and adopt Fisher's viewpoint. If we consider ourselves as valuable assets, it becomes important to seek the best "rent" for that asset. By doing so, we can generate some leftover money (after covering necessary expenses) that can be invested, thus initiating the process of compounding.

Here's the key: without maximizing the returns on our asset-ness, the process of compounding takes much longer. If we never start investing or saving, the long-term benefits will be delayed. However, by saving even small amounts of money and allowing it to compound, short-term sacrifices can transform into long-term gains. If we don't invest the money we have left after expenses, compounding simply cannot happen.

Remember, even if you're not yet wealthy, understanding the connection between wealth and income, as well as the power of compounding, can lay the foundation for a more prosperous financial future.

What Sets Billionaires, Millionaires, and the Average Person Apart?

Numerous books discuss the transition from the middle class and one of my personal favorites is Robert Kiyosaki's Rich Dad series. In my perspective, the "middle class" refers to individuals earning less than $250,000 per year. Crossing this income threshold opens up intriguing possibilities. Think of water and its different states: solid, liquid, and gas. To change its state, water requires a certain amount of energy (heat). Similarly, when we reach a threshold, remarkable transformations can occur. These opportunities are not biased toward the source of the water; it is simply the nature of things.

For employees, there are limited options to double or triple their income. Time leverage and compounding are not readily available. Aside from the occasional exceptions, such as lawyers double billing their hours, most employees have a one-to-one relationship between hours worked and dollars earned. Income increases typically stem from improved performance or adjustments for inflation. There isn't much room for significant expansion within this framework.

Our dollars need to work for us as well. By doubling the dollars we invest, we can double the returns we receive.

When individuals begin earning larger incomes, whether through high-paying employment or other business and investment ventures, they gain more choices. Savvy individuals who save money can spot opportunities that the "middle class" might miss. They can invest in real estate, stocks, or businesses. I have a friend who owned 50 fast-food restaurants and had a net worth of around $90 million. They achieved this by purchasing one asset and then reinvesting the proceeds to acquire more. This process is highly repeatable and can be applied to real estate, business acquisitions, and more. The key consideration is to focus on the net profit. Robert Kiyosaki's CashFlow game is an excellent resource for understanding the significance of investing in revenue-generating assets, which I refer to as "Money Machines."

Having managed a manufacturing facility, I am familiar with seeing rows of machines producing parts that are ultimately sold. These machines can also be considered money machines, although they don't directly generate cash. When you invest in money machines, you primarily care about the percentage of profit it produces. The higher the percentage, the more appealing it becomes to investors. Naturally, other factors such as risk and the reliability of the income are crucial in investment decisions.

Millionaires and billionaires often acquire companies. They do so because these companies generate net profit, which represents the return on investment. While this is not drastically different from buying shares in a publicly traded company, they have the advantage of purchasing the entire company and exerting more control over it. In some ways, this approach is superior to depositing money in a bank account because it can influence the rate of return, similar to earning interest. Bank accounts, on the other hand, offer little control over the rate of return.

What Do Billionaires Do?

Billionaires often invest in what can be broadly referred to as "distribution channels." The most lucrative ones are those where they have a captive audience, meaning there aren't many convenient alternatives available. For example, many seaports are privately owned, and the owners generate a steady flow of income by adding fees to access rights. The limited choices for citizens make these seaports almost monopolistic. Similarly, the land under the San Francisco airport is privately owned, and the fees charged are passed on to the airport users. Some individuals own land patents in different parts of the world and collect property taxes. Non-government corporations own utility companies, toll roads, hospitals, and other essential services, ensuring a reliable revenue stream due to the inconvenience and costliness of seeking alternatives. For instance, if you receive gas through a pipeline to your home, you are paying the service provider. Billionaires may also acquire businesses like TicketMaster, which operates as a distribution channel for entertainment, earning fees for exclusive access to certain venues. The pricing structure is usually designed to be acceptable enough to keep users within the channel.

Casinos can be seen as licensed venues for gambling, functioning as a specific channel for this activity. The profitability of casinos is evident from the buildings they own.

Acquiring these distribution channels requires significant capital. While regular individuals may buy shares in a company, the owners of distribution companies tend to enjoy better returns. Shareholders typically receive the remaining earnings of a company after expenses.

Another investment option for billionaires is to establish a private bank. Private banks must adhere to specific rules and secure sufficient startup capital to obtain their licenses. In some cases, a private bank may not have retail customers; instead, its exclusive clients are the bank's shareholders. Although it might seem odd to have your own bank with only one customer, there are significant advantages. Banks have capabilities that others do not. Fractional reserve banking, as described in historical documents, allows banks to loan out more money than they hold in deposits. This practice requires a license, which can be obtained by meeting certain capital and regulatory requirements. However, banks must adhere to the rules, or they risk losing their license.

So, how does this information help you?

1. Billionaires operate with fewer restrictions than individuals with lesser wealth. It's important to be aware of this distinction.
2. Consider the long-term perspective of wealth creation for yourself or future generations, including the possibility of owning a bank or distribution channel. Wealthy individuals often have multi-generational viewpoints.
3. Recognize how rules and regulations create advantages and disadvantages. Understanding the dynamics of the game allows you to make informed decisions based on your values and wisdom. Choose the type of business you want to engage

in wisely. For example, although you may have the opportunity to create a highly profitable online gambling system, consider the ethical implications and potential dissatisfaction that may arise from the venture.

Becoming a millionaire is within reach for many people, with over 7 million millionaires estimated to exist (excluding the value of their homes). In the internet era, individuals can achieve millionaire status in a matter of months. It's important not to despair about the distance between your current situation and your financial goals. A comfortable life can be attained without becoming a millionaire, and with discipline and proper planning. Becoming a billionaire can be a reality for you or future generations of your family but it also has the cost of becoming disconnected from reality.

The path to becoming a millionaire or billionaire largely involves following a proven process. While many people claim to offer help, not all provide the complete steps necessary to achieve success. You can find individuals who offer straightforward guidance and have a replicable system accompanied by coaching. Ultimately, it comes down to whether you are willing to follow the instructions. Although it may sound easy, many people deviate from a system due to their own "better" ideas or old conditioning that hinders their progress.

Shortcuts to Success

Successful businessmen and women understand the importance of taking efficient shortcuts. Finding better and faster ways to get things done is smart business. However, many people make the mistake of choosing the wrong shortcuts. Knowing which shortcuts to take is crucial.

Sometimes, what seems cheap can actually turn out to be expensive in the long run. Providing value is essential. If you charge money for something that lacks value, it will ultimately drain you morally. This can affect your overall well-being and wealth. True wealth, which includes experiencing joy and being open-hearted, is only possible when there's nothing to hide or feel ashamed about. Some people may be bold-faced liars, having different values and a different sense of the world. They might appear happy and successful, but their true feelings can be well-hidden, even from themselves. They develop coping skills to disconnect from those painful feelings. Nobody can truly feel good about taking advantage of others. While it might bring a temporary ego boost or sense of accomplishment, it's not a genuine feeling of inner goodness.

Chapter Summary

In this chapter, we explored the concept of wealth velocity and how it can accelerate our path to financial freedom. We learned about the incredible power of compounding, where even a small increase in the rate of return can multiply our investments over time.

By understanding the connection between wealth and income, as well as the significance of investing in revenue-generating assets, we can lay the foundation for a more prosperous financial future.

We also delved into the strategies of millionaires and billionaires, such as investing in distribution channels and acquiring businesses, which provide them with greater control and higher returns. Additionally, we discussed the importance of taking efficient shortcuts and choosing the right ones that align with our values and bring true wealth and fulfillment.

By embracing these principles and continually expanding our knowledge, we can unlock the potential to accelerate our wealth velocity and create a brighter financial future. This knowledge should expand your horizon.

10
True Wealth

All value isn't Money

Let's talk about creating true wealth—the kind that resides within us. It revolves around the feelings we carry inside. This journey is about embracing the process of being, rather than solely focusing on the destination. The journey itself is where we spend the majority of our time, while the end result is just a brief moment.

You can celebrate every accomplishment along the way. Whether it's mastering the skill of reading a business prospectus or learning to interpret stock charts on your path to financial success, each step is significant in this journey. These milestones shape who we become.

It's crucial to find joy in the process because it provides the resilience we need to push through challenging times and withstand unsolicited criticism. We should create a foundation of enjoying life and cultivate a compelling reason to put in the extra effort. Without it, we would continue to follow the same patterns as before. If we keep doing what we've always done, we'll only get more of the same. That's not true compounding.

Let me give you a non-financial example of compounding. Imagine earning an above-average income and using the free time it provides to enrich your own life or the lives of others. If your mind doubts the possibility of this, it's likely due to the limitations of past perspectives on what's considered "normal." Take a drive to a golf course in the middle of a work week, and you'll see people genuinely enjoying life and the freedom they've created.

As for me, I made plans to take professional cooking classes when I reached the age of 55. I know that it be a recreational pursuit while others may be there for career purposes. Becoming a great cook would not only be a gift to others but also an exciting adventure for me.

Remember, true wealth extends beyond financial gains. Embrace the journey, celebrate your achievements, and find joy in becoming the best version of yourself.

Wealth is like a flowing river

It's dynamic and always moving. Think of it as being alive and active. Sometimes people keep their wealth stored away, like in a bank account. But when it's just sitting there, it doesn't benefit many people. It's like having potential that hasn't been put to use. The real value lies in its movement, not in its storage.

Having money in a bank account doesn't provide much usefulness. Let's imagine a dollar bill and how it travels through the economy. As it moves from person to person, it brings life and vitality. When there's not enough money circulating, the economy becomes unhealthy. It's similar to our bodies: if our blood supply is too low, our limbs can feel pain and lack the necessary energy to function properly. They might even become weak. This is how I explain economics to people.

When there's enough money flowing, all parts of the economy receive the energy they need. They use this energy to create valuable things for the entire community.

In a reciprocal environment, when energy (money) is given, it's expected to give back something of value. These are natural laws that govern how things work. By putting your wealth into the economy (instead of a bank), you are helping yourself and others.

5% of something or 100% of zero

Let's consider the question: should I work alone or have a team?

For many years, Bill Gates indirectly managed over a thousand projects. It's impossible for one person to directly oversee so many things. While Bill had many employees, he organized them into manageable units that could be tracked. The departments were neither too large nor too small. This efficient structure is well-documented in various books and articles and serves as a blueprint for a multi-millionaire driving multiple business ideas.

Others have grown their wealth without the resources Bill Gates had. They also participated in numerous projects but didn't have complete ownership of any one project. They played a small part in efficient projects that yielded results. Not every project was successful, but they generally achieved positive outcomes because they had a strong team working with them. They shared the workload and the risks associated with failure. Overall, they saw financial progress for their contributions to each project, incrementally.

I've observed individuals who work alone and have complete ownership of their projects. However, these one-person ventures often take longer to complete and may not be as good due to the limited perspective. While it's true that Edison may not have created the light bulb if he had listened to others too much, he still collaborated with a team. If I had limited time to produce something, I would achieve better results by collaborating with others on teams. Working on a project alone would either lead to 100% completion or total incompleteness. Incompleteness doesn't yield any results; I can't rent out an unfinished house. However, if I had a stake in many houses and some of them were rentable, I would generate income. I would prefer to have 5% ownership in 20 projects rather than 100% ownership of an incomplete project.

Wanting to be "the one" who did it all is driven by ego. Being the sole person responsible for a single project is a financial risk. Putting all your eggs in one basket prevents the creation of multiple income streams. There is the additional risk of a team that is out-building the one person and gets the focus and success from finishing first.

Having multiple projects and being the only person managing them is even worse. Our focus becomes divided. If the projects are small enough to be reasonably completed and generate income without constant attention, then managing multiple small projects can work well. However, this scenario is not common. Typically, there's something that requires ongoing attention to generate income. It's similar to an airplane trying to take off—it needs to reach a specific speed. Anything below that speed is like driving at high speed on a limited-distance road.

The best approach is to relax and carefully choose projects based on risk and reward ratios. Ask yourself, "Can I really make money here?" and then find people who want to join you on that journey. One of the challenging aspects for me is saying "no" to other ideas, as they can be distractions. I focus on my few favorite projects where I excel and skip all the other enticing opportunities. It's hard to accept that I can't do everything I want, but it's true. Therefore, I must prioritize to achieve success.

It's also beneficial to receive income from multiple sources. During times of economic change, one industry often thrives while another falters. Diversification ensures a balanced income even during slow economic periods.

Easy Tools to support your journey

Managing personal finance and planning for retirement involves various aspects. Here are some types of tools that can help in these areas:

Expense Tracking apps

It's never been easier to track expenses. Here's a sample of one in action. The tiny effort it takes to track the expenses reveals very useful insights. And the app does the heavy lifting for you.

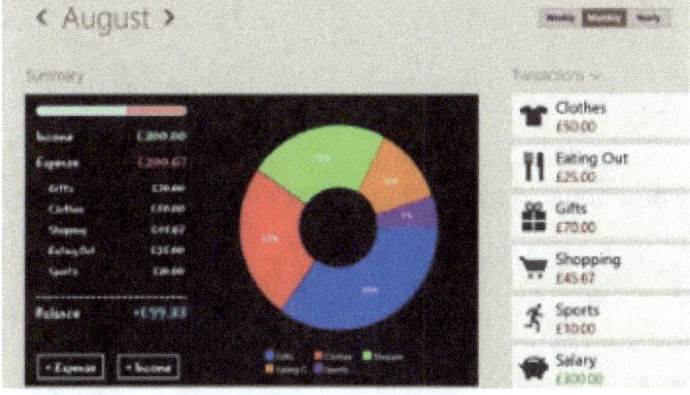

Budgeting apps

Budgeting tools help you create and manage a budget. It's better if the app connects your expenses to your budget. Then you can see variances, or even better self-control on spending: "I can't go there this month 'cause I've spent too much on that already." Popular options include Mint, YNAB (You Need a Budget), and Personal Capital.

Retirement Planning Calculators

Retirement calculators allow you to estimate how much you need to save for retirement and determine the optimal contribution amount. Tools like Fidelity's Retirement Calculator, Vanguard Retirement Nest Egg Calculator, and AARP Retirement Calculator can provide insights into your retirement savings goals. Their purpose is to show you how much you'll need to put into investments per month to reach a goal. The alternative is to lower your expectations for retirement. The challenge is guessing how long you'll live. This is where you'll see the power of compounding working for you. This demonstrates the importance of seeking a better-than-average rate of return on your money.

Financial Education Platforms

Websites and apps like Investopedia, Khan Academy, and Morningstar offer educational resources, articles, and courses on personal finance, investing, and retirement planning.

Stock and Crypto Communities

I've worked with the people at www.Terrasoari.com and they have an online community and some stock trading and alert tools. They are honest and helpful.

Investment Management Platforms

These platforms help you manage your investments, monitor their performance, and track your portfolio allocation. Examples include online brokerage platforms like Vanguard and Charles Schwab/TD Ameritrade. You can set alerts and review your ownership in stocks. They won't tell you what or when to buy shares. This should be done by yourself with simple tools and strategies and help from online communities (mentioned above).

Social Security Calculators

If you're eligible for Social Security benefits, these calculators help you estimate your future benefits based on your earnings history and retirement age. The official Social Security Administration website offers a retirement estimator tool.

Tax Planning Software

Tools like TurboTax and H&R Block provide guidance and assistance in preparing and filing your tax returns, maximizing deductions, and optimizing your tax situation.

Remember, it's essential to research and choose tools that align with your specific financial goals and personal circumstances. It may also be helpful to consult with a financial advisor for personalized guidance on your retirement planning journey.

Simplest Budget Management

This is my tried-and-true approach that I've been using for most of my life, and it's all about being simple and practical. At the start of each month, I withdraw the exact amount of spending cash I'll need, making sure it fits within my budget. I've already taken care of my usual monthly expenses by leaving that money in my bank account. I've even transferred some extra cash to a separate account specifically for unexpected costs like dental or car repairs. The spending money I have is right in my wallet, so I can easily see how much I have and decide how to spend it.

This approach saves me time too since I only visit the bank once per month. This system works because I've made a list of my regular expenses and even saved up for those irregular ones, which means I don't have to stress about meeting my basic needs. However, some places prefer electronic payments instead of cash. So I also have a debit card with some spending money set aside for those situations.

The great thing is, I don't have to meticulously track every small expense I make. I've developed some habits when it comes to spending money, and I'm always conscious of how much "free money" I have left.

When I had a job that paid me every two weeks, it didn't always align with the start of the month. During those years, I followed my monthly routine but only relied on two paychecks each month. However, whenever there was an extra paycheck, I saw it as a bonus and put it towards savings or used it for special occasions like birthday gifts.

Now, let's talk about car insurance. Instead of paying it monthly and incurring interest fees of around 13%, I decided to tackle it differently. Car insurance is due once a year, so I would assign one of those extra paychecks specifically for that purpose. Why would I want to pay the insurance company so much in interest fees when I could avoid it? Many people simply pay their insurance monthly without realizing that those seemingly small fees can really add up over the years.

By being mindful of my pay schedule and taking advantage of the extra paychecks, I was able to make smarter financial decisions and save money in the long run. It's all about finding ways to optimize your finances and avoid unnecessary costs.

In a nutshell, I've found a practical way to manage my finances that helps me stay on top of my expenses and gives me peace of mind without feeling overwhelmed.

The Journey to True Wealth

We have explored the concept of true wealth and its significance beyond mere monetary gains. We have learned that the journey itself holds immense value, as it is where we spend the majority of our time.

Throughout our discussion, we have emphasized the importance of finding joy in the process and celebrating every accomplishment along the way. Whether it is mastering a new skill or pursuing a passion, each step we take shapes our character and contributes to our personal growth.

So far in this book, we have also delved into the idea of compounding, showcasing its effects not only in the realm of finances but also in our overall well-being when we reach retirement age. By nurturing our own happiness and embracing experiences that enrich our lives, we create a foundation of resilience that helps us navigate through challenging times.

Additionally, we have explored the analogy of wealth as a flowing river, emphasizing the importance of allowing our resources to circulate and benefit not only ourselves but also the wider community. We have seen that true value lies in movement, not in stagnation.

In considering the question of working alone versus collaborating with a team, we have examined the benefits of teamwork, sharing the workload, and reducing the risks of failure. We have learned that diversifying our income streams and avoiding sole reliance on one venture is crucial for long-term financial stability.

To support our journey, we have discussed various practical tools and resources. From expense tracking and budgeting apps to retirement planning calculators and investment management platforms, these tools can assist us in managing our personal finances and planning for the future. It's never been easier to stay on target. And there is an online community that is supportive too.

Chapter Summary

As we conclude this chapter, let us remember that true wealth extends far beyond financial gains. It resides within us and is nurtured through the joy we find in our pursuits, the resilience we build, and the contributions we make to the world around us. Embrace the journey, celebrate your achievements, and strive to become the best version of yourself, knowing that your true wealth lies in the experiences and the growth you cultivate along the way.

11
Success and Failure

Success Leaves Clues

When people succeed there are usually common threads to their success. "Clues" for a repeatable pattern.

Here are some summaries that provide a brief overview of the career and financial opinions offered by a few notably successful individuals. They have shared a wealth of knowledge and insights through various platforms, including books, interviews, and speeches. Exploring their public comments can provide a general comprehensive understanding of their opinions and perspectives. This is just my summary so you can decide whom to follow more exactly. This is divided into Career and Financial opinions and remember these are not exact quotes but just summaries. You can see a common thread in these summaries.

Elon Musk:
Career opinions: Elon Musk, the visionary behind Tesla and SpaceX, encourages others to pursue ambitious goals and take risks in their careers. Find something meaningful that has the potential to make a positive impact on the world. Be persistent, resilient, and willing to learn from failures, as they are stepping stones toward success. Follow your passion and strive to make a difference in an industry that excites you.

Financial opinions: Elon Musk's financial opinions revolve around thinking long-term and investing in opportunities that have the potential for significant growth. Be prudent with your financial decisions, focus on saving, and avoid unnecessary debt. Consider investing in innovative and sustainable industries that align with your values and have the potential to generate substantial returns in the future. He sold PayPal for $1.5 billion, but didn't have enough funds to build Tesla in the beginning. He was rescued by other wealthy people. This reflects the need to work in partnerships and watch debt levels.

Simon Sinek:
Career opinions: Simon Sinek, a renowned author and motivational speaker, advises us to discover our "why" or purpose. Explore your passions, values, and what drives you. Find a career that aligns with

your values and allows you to make a positive impact. Build strong relationships, nurture trust, and collaborate with others. Remember that success is not just about individual achievements but also about contributing to something larger than yourself.

Financial opinions: Simon Sinek's financial opinions focuses on being mindful of your spending habits and making informed financial decisions. Develop healthy financial habits, such as budgeting, saving, and avoiding unnecessary expenses. Consider the long-term implications of your financial choices and prioritize investments that align with your values and goals. Seek financial education and learn to make your money work for you through strategies like saving, investing, and diversifying your income. I personally really enjoy the way he speaks.

Steve Jobs:
Career opinions: Steve Jobs, the visionary co-founder of Apple, encourages us to follow our passion in our careers. Find something you love and believe in, as passion is key to overcoming challenges and achieving extraordinary results. Combine your interests and talents to create something unique and meaningful. Embrace continuous learning and personal growth, and never settle for mediocrity. Have faith in your abilities and keep pushing your boundaries. When he had setbacks he just went a different route: Pixar is a shining example of moving on.

Financial opinions: Steve Jobs' financial advice emphasizes the importance of financial discipline and a long-term perspective. Be mindful of your spending habits, differentiate between needs and wants, and save money regularly. Invest in your own skills and education to increase your earning potential. Consider the value of delayed gratification and make wise financial decisions that align with your long-term goals. Build a strong foundation of financial knowledge and seek opinions from trusted sources to make informed choices.

Richard Branson:
Career opinions: Richard Branson, the entrepreneur behind the Virgin Group, advises us to be open to new opportunities and take calculated

risks in our careers. Embrace your entrepreneurial spirit and don't be afraid to explore unconventional paths. Surround yourself with talented and passionate people who inspire and challenge you. Maintain a positive attitude, persevere through challenges, and always seek a healthy work-life balance. I happen to know that he takes personal development workshops and loves to grow as a person. You'd think he'd quit after reaching obvious success levels. The inner story is also important to him.

Financial opinions: Richard Branson's financial opinions organized around taking calculated risks and seeking financial opportunities. Be willing to invest in innovative ideas and ventures that align with your values and have the potential for growth. Emphasize the importance of financial literacy and seek knowledge to make informed financial decisions. Maintain a healthy balance between spending, saving, and investing. Focus on building a diverse portfolio and be mindful of potential risks and rewards.

Summary:
Remember, these are simplified summaries of the advice given by these leaders. You may have noticed that they all have similar themes. It's important to continue learning, seeking guidance from trusted sources, and tailoring opinions to your personal circumstances and goals.

Failure Stories

There are many stories online about famous people that failed. We can learn from those stories, without being worried ourselves.

I have the following true story I learned from high-end accountants I've worked with. This is about fancy footwork by accountants and lawyers. None of this applies to simply holding things in your own name or your business's name. The balance of this chapter most people can skip and go straight to the chapter summary and feel like they're not missing out. For the very curious-minded, this chapter includes advanced tactics with money in these next sections.

How One Billionaire Failed

Running a successful business means working with accountants, which is pretty normal. As your business makes more money, it's smart to find legal ways to organize your finances to fit the rules. It might seem strange that classifying something differently can affect the taxes you owe, even though you're still earning the same amount of money. But if we try to make too much sense of it, we'll just end up frustrated or chaotic.

Right now, society's understanding of "society" and profit is in a certain place. Thankfully, in the future, we'll likely reevaluate these concepts with better moral values. But we're not there yet.

An accountant's job is basically to organize things into specific categories and make persuasive arguments to justify them. This helps lower the taxes owed by the business owner, which means more money in their pocket after paying the accountants. The more money they save, the quicker the business owner can become wealthier.

However, accountants and tax lawyers don't know everything, and they don't have control over the system. They have a duty to the system itself, so they normally won't take you to places you might want to go. But sometimes they're unaware of obvious things too.

In most countries, lawyers take an oath to the State or Head of State. The State is their top allegiance and where they get their license to practice. Their second duty is to the accounting or law society, not the regular society we usually think of. Their society consists of the people who supervise them. Lastly, these licensed practitioners always have an implied duty to their business or practice; otherwise, they won't stay in business.

Since we aren't part of their top priorities, we can hope to receive good care as their fourth priority. It's possible to get good service as long as our agenda doesn't conflict with their top three priorities (but keep in mind that not all accountants or lawyers are the same). If you're looking for a great lawyer or accountant, here are two tips: First, ask people you know about the practitioners they use and the actual results they've achieved (not just the promises). Second, when you meet with a practitioner, ask them directly, "Will you work in my best interest?" If they hesitate or show uncertainty, they're probably not the right fit.

In my experiences working with some of the best accountants, I've come across some interesting stories. Let me share one about a billionaire from Hong Kong. He wasn't a citizen or resident of the country he planned to move to, so he hired a well-known accounting firm. They set up a few trusts before he arrived in the new country, and everything was done legally. After he settled in, he bought a multimillion-dollar house. Eventually, the tax authorities sent him paperwork stating their opinion on how things should be assessed for tax purposes. He disagreed with their assessment and relied on his reputable accountants. Surprisingly, the tax authorities seized his house.

When I first heard this story, like most people, I thought it couldn't be right. However, it taught me an important lesson. The ruling government of a country makes the rules, and if you give them exclusive jurisdiction, you don't have many options. The key question to ask is: What did the billionaire do wrong?

It's important to observe what works and what doesn't while maintaining a healthy skepticism toward what people tell you. The main takeaway from the story is that the tax authorities have the power to interpret and enforce their own definitions. For example, the term "Trust" has a specific meaning in tax laws around the world, while "Foundation" may not be as commonly defined. The billionaire had a Trust, not a Foundation. And that means all the difference, just as the words are different, their implications are different too. This is why you hire experts but also need to review the work they do for you.

For Wanna-be Billionaires

A registered Trust is not an entity but rather a relationship (or a financial instrument). When someone has a registered Trust, it's like having a football in the air.

Imagine you're watching a soccer game, and the referee has the power to decide if a goal is valid or not; but as in the tax department case, decided the outcome before the ball lands. With this referee, when a player kicks the ball toward the net, the referee can make the call while the ball is still in the air or after it has been received by another player. When it comes to trusts and foundations, the judge that works with the tax authorities has the authority to determine how the money and assets within the Trust should be treated. Basically, they decide who caught the uncaught ball and thus will pay the taxes and penalties.

In different countries like Switzerland, USA, and Canada, there have been cases where judges have decided who should be responsible for the income and assets in a trust: the trustee (person managing the trust), the grantor (person who created the trust), or beneficiary (person who benefits from the trust). These judges often use the 'principle of transparency' as their basis for making these decisions. Even if the local laws don't specifically define trust, the judge may still apply this principle. The important thing to remember is that trusts may not always protect your interests if it goes against what the tax authorities want. It's better to have clear rules that everyone follows to avoid arguments in life, just like how being offside in soccer has clear rules.

Now, let's talk briefly about foundations. A foundation is like an organization with its own identity. Famous families like the Rockefellers, Gates, and Fords have foundations named after them, such as the Rockefeller Foundation and Ford Foundation. If a foundation owns something, like a property that generates income, legally it belongs to the foundation. However, the tax authorities in your country may still want to attribute that income to you if you are the beneficiary of the foundation. It's their job to collect as much money as possible, so they'll use any means necessary for their job. In many countries, the tax agents even get bonuses, promotions, or some recognition based on how much money they bring in. They have the authority, rules, motivation, and support of the courts. So, why would you want to fight against all of that?

In summary, the referee (courtroom judge) has the power to make decisions about trusts and foundations. Trusts can be tricky because they may not always work in your favor when it comes to taxes. Foundations, on the other hand, are like organizations that can own assets and generate income, but the tax authorities might still try to attribute it to you. It's often better to follow clear rules and avoid unnecessary conflicts with the authorities.

Chapter Summary

In this chapter, we explore the opinions of successful individuals and learn valuable lessons about career and financial success. We delve into the wisdom of Elon Musk, Simon Sinek, Steve Jobs, and Richard Branson, who have shared their insights through various platforms. Each person emphasizes the importance of finding purpose and passion in your career, being persistent and resilient, and making a positive impact on the world. They also highlight the significance of long-term thinking, prudent financial decisions, and investing in opportunities that align with your values.

The chapter also touches on failure stories and provides a cautionary tale about relying solely on accountants and lawyers for financial planning. It reminds us that accountants and lawyers have certain priorities and obligations, which may not always align with our best interests. The story of a billionaire who faced unexpected tax consequences demonstrates the importance of understanding the rules and being cautious when it comes to trust and foundation structures. I suggest seeking expert guidance while maintaining a healthy skepticism. It's important to stay within and follow clear rules to avoid unnecessary conflicts with tax authorities. Fancy footwork gets tripped up easily.

Success is a journey, and it requires continuous learning, adapting, and making informed decisions. By learning from the experiences of successful individuals and being aware of potential pitfalls, you can navigate your career and financial path more effectively.

12
Final Thoughts

Quick Insights

Here are some fast facts that will get you thinking: All business skills can be learned. There are numerous books available that provide valuable information about various industries and business skills. However, most people only read a single book cover to cover. And only 1% of individuals are wealthy by the time they reach 65.

Here are a few more fast facts: High earners generally provide 10% more value to the customer than average earners but often have double the income; from giving above-average service. The same principle applies to business services and products. Furthermore, 80% of self-made millionaires started and established their own businesses.

If you don't have a business yet, choose an industry that aligns with your lifestyle and has a good potential for profitability. Pursue a vocation that ignites your passion because it becomes easier to go the extra mile in delivering excellence. Having a remarkable service or product will help your reputation spread through word of mouth, propelling you further and faster.

Before diving in, identify your competitive edge to avoid competing solely on price. Remember that 90% of successful businesses are started by skilled and experienced individuals. And if things don't work out right away, don't be disheartened because almost nothing succeeds on the first try. It's true that 80% of businesses fail in their first 5 years. This just proves your idea needs adjustments or is what the marketplace wanted. Look for a problem that needs to be solved for people, and offer the solution.

If your business is stuck, there is help available to get you unstuck. However, do thorough research on potential coaches before investing in one. Ensure they have a proven track record of success in their respective field and aren't simply skilled at selling themselves. It's essential to have a contract that clearly defines the specific outcomes you expect from the coaching relationship, with measurable targets.

If you want to reach your goals faster, be aware that top performers hire competent coaches. For example, Tiger Woods relied on multiple golf coaches. Contrary to popular belief, they are the best not solely on skill but **because** they also have coaches. Coaches can help individuals achieve their aspirations within a single lifetime. This concept is comparable to an airplane needing to reach a certain velocity before the runway ends; otherwise, it won't take flight.

When a fish is unwell in an aquarium, the common remedy is to change the water. Similarly, if the environment around you is hindering your success, make changes.

Final Thoughts on Making Choices

In the realm of engineering, the most significant mistakes occur or are prevented during the design stage. If a mistake goes unnoticed during the design phase, it requires at least ten times more effort to rectify it later.

Consider the width of roads, which is largely influenced by the ancient practice of two horses pulling a wagon. This historical design choice still impacts the size of objects that can be transported by land, even affecting the transportation of Space Shuttle components. The design of roads is unlikely to change significantly after millions of miles have already been paved. Naturally, the design of the road width wasn't thought into the future needs. The design was a destination only, not future thinking.

Sometimes, our habits become incorporated into the design of our choices, deeply ingrained and pervasive. Unlike rigid pavement, our minds and habits are more adaptable. The future remains unpaved, offering endless possibilities. However, our habits can create deep ruts, restricting our potential for growth and change.

Birds effortlessly soar through the sky, flowers naturally bloom, and butterflies undergo remarkable transformations without consciously contemplating their actions. It is only when we experience pain that its reality becomes tangible. We may not perceive ourselves as changing, but every cell in our body is replaced every few years. The old cells provide instructions to the new ones, dictating their appearance and location. This process is a form of change, akin to a changing of the guard, rather than a noticeable improvement. Without the renewal of cells, our existence would cease after a few years.

Within ourselves we witness multiple perspectives coexisting (mind and body), each holding its own truth. Cells attend to themselves mostly without our attention. Our old habits or some new thoughts could become habits that look after themselves without attention. Except habits guide our future more significantly than renewed skin cells.

Using reflection on habits and failures gives a useful perspective. The perspective serves as intelligence for the direction we choose to face next.

And what will you put in your schedule? Thoughts are "things" but they only come to life when they are actioned into a schedule. That's what I found out in my thirties.

Achieving Abundance

These next steps represent the harmonization of ancient principles with contemporary business practices, resulting in a powerful framework for success. Together, they form harmonious pairs that foster abundance. It is recommended to pair them as follows:

1. Conduct thorough research and initiate action.
2. Show genuine care for others and excel in administrative/managerial roles.
3. Voice your aspirations and embrace a mindset of growth.
4. Establish a systematic approach and generate results within that framework.
5. Cultivate an abundance mentality and delegate tasks to others.

Final Reflections

Life is not a battle to be won, but a series of paths to be explored. Each individual's journey is unique, with their own set of decisions to be made and actions to be taken. You have endured challenges and emerged stronger, demonstrating your resilience.

Can you sense the joy that resides within you? If not, perhaps it's time to seek it out. The pursuit of happiness is distinct from actually experiencing happiness. It is important to recognize that wealth does not guarantee happiness; many affluent individuals still feel a void within themselves. If you can fill that void with something truly fulfilling from within, then the pursuit of wealth can become a rewarding endeavor.

In essence, you have already achieved victory. It's not a battle, but an adventure. The way we navigate this journey is where our life truly unfolds. The attainment of wealth becomes a grand celebration, but it no longer holds the power to dictate our happiness. With this perspective, wealth is more likely to come, yet its presence or absence becomes inconsequential. Ultimately, you can choose to live in a state of happiness, independent of external circumstances.

My goal for this book was to share the knowledge and insights gained over the years so you don't need as many 'face slaps' from life.

I wish you the best. Stay Curious.

Appendix - Action

We all want results. As a friend in marketing slyly says "117% of men want more money."

You're the primary hero in the story of your life. Here is a quick review of things you could take action on:

1. In today's dollars, **how much do you need** per month if you didn't go to work?

2. Use online tools to find out **how much you need to save and when you can retire** to enjoy a comfortable life without income. Prepare to be amazed and maybe a little worried by what you discover.

3. Now that you have this knowledge, it's time to think about **your spending, income, and investments**. How can you achieve financial freedom?

4. Start by creating a **time budget to prioritize activities** that will secure your future.

5. It's also important to define who you are and who you want to become. Make a **declaration about your goals and aspirations**.

6. Think about the people who will support you in making the necessary changes. Who can **be on your team** to help you reach your financial goals?

7. Surround yourself with positive influences that can inspire you to **make changes in your career and investments**.

8. **Create a schedule** for the week where you set time aside for your achieving goals by reading and planning and mindfully making adjustments. As captain of your ship, you need to spend time in the navigation.

9. Put **something on your phone** that propels you to your positive life story. Give that attention along with the usual time-filling habits.

Acknowledgments and Thanks

First, I'd like to give thanks to the Beta Readers: Tanya Carrum and Natalia D. Their quick feedback confirmed I was on the right path and this would be helpful to readers.

Rina Forristal, a very bright university student, provided the far better title we have here. The working title was Money School and you can see her recommendation was a big improvement.

Proofreading and editing were graciously provided by Susan Pratt and Rina Forristal. Both are excellent at providing editing and feedback to make this book better. Susan was a professor in foreign countries for many years and also helped immensely with a previous book I wrote for beginning investors "Profit in Pajamas". Teamwork is a source of joy and inspiration.

Formatting and Illustrations are by Adin770 at Fiverr.com. They're my go-to source for all formatting.

My long-term friends Jim Short and Murray McAllindon, also gave feedback on the book, but more importantly have been there when I truly needed a friend. And every other day too. I could never say enough.

www.ingramcontent.com/pod-product-compliance
Lightning Source LLC
Chambersburg PA
CBHW070031300526
45794CB00001B/453